SPRINT

YOUR WAY TO

SCRUM

50 Practical Tips to Accelerate Your Scrum

Bonsy Yelsangi, CST
Valerio Zanini, CST, CPIT

5D Vision Publishing

Sprint Your Way to Scrum: 50 Practical Tips to Accelerate Your Scrum

Printed in the United States of America

10 9 8 7 6 5 4 3 2 1

ISBN (Paperback): 9780998985466
ISBN (Hardcover): 9780998985473
ISBN (E-Book): 9780998985480

We plant one tree for every copy of this book sold, in partnership with ForestPlanet.org

Cover design by Marko Bijelic - marko@hipinspire.com
Photos and illustrations: Freepik - Freepik.com Premium License

SPRINT

YOUR WAY TO

SCRUM

Includes an interview with Jeff Sutherland,
co-creator of Scrum

Bonsy Yelsangi, CST
Valerio Zanini, CST, CPIT

Praise for Sprint Your Way to Scrum

Since 1993 when the first Scrum team increased velocity by 500% in the third sprint I have been helping create hyperproductive teams. It is very hard to do this without expert training and coaching. In fact, the best data on Agile teams show only 42% are successful and the other 58% are late, over budget, with unhappy customers or deliver nothing. Clearly, people have a lot of questions that need good answers to turn these failing teams into a success story. Valerio has completed our Registered Scrum Training Program by spending a week working with me and I know he knows all the tips and tricks for enabling great teams. Reading through this book you will find consistently good advice for tackling some of your toughest problems. I recommend it.

Jeff Sutherland

Co-creator of Scrum, Author of "Scrum: The Art of Doing Twice the Work in Half the Time"

Bonsy and Valerio have done an excellent job collecting the top 50 questions most asked about scrum, and provided a wealth of real-world answers, case studies and examples. This book would be a valued reference book on any scrum master's desk, helping to address most common situations.

Howard Sublett

CEO Scrum Alliance

Sprint Your Way to Scrum is the perfect companion for change leaders on their agile journey. Packed with practical and challenging scenarios you're destined to face along the way, Bonsy Yelsangi and Valerio Zanini provide expert advice, relevant guidance and a healthy share of real-life experience to help you conquer the most common obstacles on your path. This book is not only essential as an effective "impediments remover", it is a highly enjoyable read that I am confident you'll want to keep nearby and easily accessible for the long haul. Highly recommended!

Jorgen Hesselberg

Co-founder Comparative Agility, Author of "Unlocking Agility"

This book is a great resource for Scrum Masters and Agile Coaches looking for quick answers to some of the most frequently asked questions beginners have when it comes to implementing Scrum. The in-the-trenches experience of the authors is reflected in the straightforward, down to earth answer they give to each question and the real life stories sprinkled throughout the book. For more advanced coaches, it is a good read to gain perspectives on how other experienced professionals approach some of the most common challenges we face on a daily basis with our teams. I felt engaged reading it and found myself wanting to answer some of these questions myself!

Xavier Quesada Allué

Certified Scrum Trainer (CST), Managing Partner at Agilar, President of Agile Spain

"Easy to learn", says Scrum co-inventor Ken Schwaber, "But difficult to master." With clarity and insight, Bonsy and Valerio have illuminated a path to mastery that is both practical and inspiring. The experiences of these two expert Scrum teachers leaps off of each page and imparts sage advice that has taken years to acquire. Savor and apply this gem of a book and take your scrum team from good to great!

Kert Peterson
Certified Scrum Trainer (CST), Accredited Kanban Trainer (AKT)

Bonsy and Valerio have compiled a treasure chest of insightful answers to the most common questions from students, practitioners and leaders in pursuit of leveraging Scrum to be more Agile. Since I helped them both on their journeys to achieving the elite Certified Scrum Trainer designation, I'm incredibly proud of them for the clarity and detail of what they have written. Bonsy and Valerio have elaborated key concepts in an accessible format that I plan to share as a resource with my students and clients.

Jason Tanner
Certified Scrum Trainer (CST), CEO Applied Frameworks

Every day, many business and technology leaders make mistakes that cost them thousands if not millions of dollars in the quest for agility and organizational effectiveness. This book changes that by sharing simple solutions and real life stories for common team and organization impediments that can be leveraged by product owners and scrum masters alike in every organization.

Anil Jaising
Certified Scrum Trainer (CST), Chief Product Owner at Concepts & Beyond

TABLE OF CONTENTS

INTRODUCTION

HOW WILL THIS BOOK BENEFIT YOU?

According to the modern-day philosopher and investor Naval Ravikant, "To write a great book, you must first become the book."

This book comes from our direct experience working with Scrum Teams and especially from teaching Scrum to thousands of professionals around the world. We have collected 50 of the most asked questions about Scrum. We ourselves had these questions when we were playing one of the roles on the Scrum Team at different stages of our careers.

This book is not an analysis or a research paper on Scrum, but it is a practical list of tips and techniques – a handy toolbox that will help you and your peers in implementing the Scrum framework effectively. It will help you get a buy-in from your team members to use Scrum because it will provide you ways in which to educate them and to answer the questions they always seem to have about Scrum.

Scrum is the most widely adopted Agile framework in the world. It is easy to understand and yet, difficult to master.

Having trained thousands of professionals across the world and helped them implement Scrum in their organizations, we provide practical, succinct, and effective answers to 50 of the most common questions about Scrum. There is not a right way or the only way to implement Scrum. In these pages we list the various ways in which we have helped teams organize their work and have fun while doing so.

This book is for Scrum Practitioners, Scrum Masters, Product Owners, and Agile Coaches who want to refine their expertise and to take Scrum to the next level.

We are teachers at heart, and cannot imagine not sharing the knowledge we have accumulated over our many years of teaching. By firsthand experience, we know that there are many of you who have these 50 questions and are seeking an answer.

This book is based on our experience, told in our own words and candidly, in our own style.

We hope that you find value in these pages and that it brings joy in your work and in your life.

THE SCRUM FRAMEWORK

Scrum is an Agile framework for developing new products and for extending existing ones. It is one of the most common frameworks implemented in Agile. It has been around since the early 1990s, and provides a repeatable, consistent, and effective set of events to help development teams build products.

Scrum is not, by itself, a technique that is utilized to build products; rather, it provides the framework that enables teams to collaborate and to follow a set of rules. Teams can then employ the specific techniques that are most suitable to designing and to developing their products.

Scrum is easy to understand yet difficult to master. It exists when applied in its entirety (roles, events, artifacts, and simple rules, as defined by the Scrum Guide).

Scrum enables teams to build products using an iterative, incremental, and adaptive process, therefore reducing risk and improving the outcome. It reduces the cost of changing and of adapting the plan to varying requirements or to customer needs, and therefore reduces the overall risk of the project.

Work is usually done in multiple iterations of the same duration. During each iteration, the team builds a piece of the product, tests it, and collects feedback from stakeholders. The team then prepares to work on the next iteration and repeats the process until the full product is completed.

Because Scrum offers multiple opportunities for inspecting the work and for collecting feedback, it allows teams to validate their product along the way, or quickly change course if needed.

In its essence, Scrum is composed of 5 events, 3 roles, and 3 artifacts:

EVENTS

Sprint, Sprint Planning, Daily Scrum, Sprint Review, and Sprint Retrospective

ROLES

Scrum Master, Product Owner, and Developers

ARTIFACTS

Product Backlog, Sprint Backlog, and Increment

Key Concepts

- Scrum is a framework, not a methodology or a technique.

- Scrum can be extended with practices and with techniques as needed by the team.

- Scrum is iterative, incremental, and adaptive.

- Work is done in iterations of 1 month or less, called "Sprints."

- Each iteration builds an Increment of a working product.

- Each Increment is fully done at the end of each Sprint, requiring no extra work or rework to complete it.

- Feedback and validation are collected at least for each iteration.

- There are only 3 roles in Scrum

LEARN MORE

1. What is Scrum? - https://www.5dvision.com/post/what-is-scrum/

2. Scrum Guide - https://scrumguides.org/

Scrum Workflow

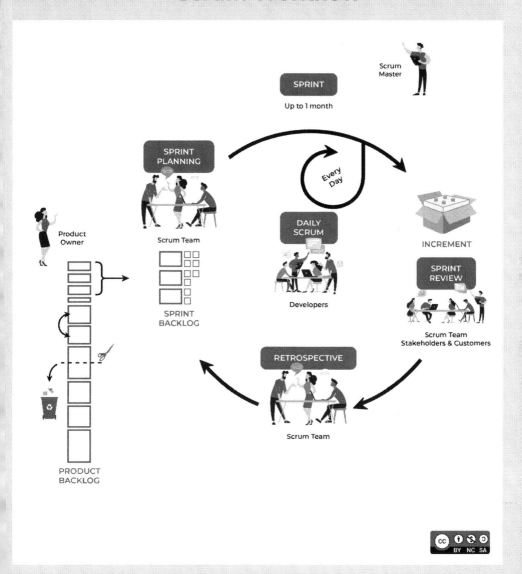

Overview of the 5 Scrum Events

What is Scrum?

	Sprint	Sprint Planning	Daily Scrum	Sprint Review	Retrospective
Timebox	1 month or less	8 hours (*)	15 min	4 hours (*)	3 hours (*)
Purpose	Build a product incrementally and iteratively. Improve predictability and consistency. The Sprint is a container for the other 4 Scrum events.	Define the Sprint Goal, select the work to do in the Sprint from the Product Backlog, and plan the work. Ensure a sustainable pace.	Inspect progress towards the Sprint Goal and adapt the plan daily. Create transparency on any impediments.	For the stakeholders to inspect the Increment, provide feedback on work done, and decide next steps or whether to release.	Support continuous improvement for the Scrum Team. Find ways to improve team productivity, product quality, and team happiness.
Participants	Everyone involved in the product development together with the Scrum Team	Scrum Team (SMEs optional)	Developers (SM and PO optional)	Scrum Team + Stakeholders.	Scrum Team.
Outcomes	Completed product Increment(s) for the Sprint, and feedback on the work done.	Sprint Backlog with plan for the work to do in the Sprint and Sprint Goal.	Team alignment, adaptation of plan, impediments.	Feedback and validation, updates to the Product Backlog, decision to release.	Improvement to work process, tools, DoD, and team health
Do it right	Sprint duration is fixed by Scrum Team and then stays the same for all Sprints. The work selected for a Sprint should be completely done by the end of the Sprint.	PO sets the why. PO and Developers decide the what. Developers set the how and how much (capacity) for the Sprint.	The Developers review the progress on the work and update their plan to achieve the Sprint Goal.	PO and Developers conduct together. This is not just a "demo". Opportunity to update Product Backlog and discuss release plan.	Opportunity for continuous improvement. Identify 1 or 2 issues to solve with the team, and plan to work on them in the next Sprint (action items).

(*) Max timebox for a 1-month Sprint. Timebox is usually shorter for shorter Sprints

Sprint

Timebox

Timebox length for a 1-month Sprint? Does it change for shorter Sprints?

- Up to 1 month in duration
- The duration of a Sprint is always the same

Empiricism

Timebox length for a 1-month Sprint? Does it change for shorter Sprints?

- Sprints ensure that, at least once per Sprint, stakeholders inspect the Increment, and the Scrum Team adapts its plan based on what it learns.
- Transparency is increased as a result of collaboration.

Purpose

Why do we do this? What do we get out of it?

- Incremental and iterative development of a product while minimizing risks and maximizing opportunity for learning.
- Improve predictability and consistency.

Scrum Master

What's their role at this event?

Work with the Scrum Team to adopt Scrum effectively, help remove impediments, and increase the team's productivity

Product Owner

What's their role at this event?

- Maximize the value of the work done by the Scrum Team.
- Only the Product Owner can decide to cancel a Sprint, when its goal becomes obsolete.

Developers

What's their role at this event?

Deliver an Increment of functionality that is usable and satisfies the Definition of Done.

Inputs

What are the inputs to this event?

Ordered Product Backlog, Product Goal, previous Increments, Definition of Done.

Outcomes

What are the possible outcomes of the event?

- Increment, feedback and validation, updated Product Backlog, opportunities for team improvement

Sprint Planning

Timebox

Timebox length for a 1-month Sprint? Does it change for shorter Sprints?

· Up to 8 hours for 1-month Sprints.
· Usually shorter for shorter Sprints.

Empiricism

How does this event support inspection and adaption and increase transparency?

· Each Sprint has its own Sprint Goal and Sprint Backlog.
· The work selected from the Product Backlog aligns with the Sprint Goal.
· The team's available capacity is adjusted based on inspection of previous performance.

Purpose

Why do we do this? What do we get out of it?

· Create the Sprint Backlog: Define the goal for the Sprint (WHY).
· Select the PBIs that the Developers can deliver by the end of the Sprint (WHAT) and create a plan for how to get the work done (HOW).
· Ensure sustainable pace of work for the Developers.

Scrum Master

What's their role at this event?

· Ensure the meeting takes place and that everyone understands its purpose and their role in it.
· May facilitate the event if needed so that its goal can be achieved.
· Coach the Developers on how to select the WHAT and organize the HOW.

Product Owner

What's their role at this event?

During "WHY"
· Provide input to Sprint Goal.
· Align to overall Product Goal.

During "WHAT"
Provide context and priorities for selection of PBIs by Developers.

During "HOW"
Answer questions and help Developers if needed.

Developers

What's their role at this event?

During "WHY"
Negotiate with the Product Owner the goal of the Sprint.

During "WHAT"
Select the work to be done in the Sprint to achieve the Goal. Confirm it fits within available capacity.

During "HOW"
Break-down the work and prepare a plan on how to get the work completed during the Sprint.

Inputs

What are the inputs to this event?

Ordered Product Backlog, overall Product Goal, Definition of Done, team's historical velocity, planned vacations or events that may affect capacity for the Sprint.

Outcomes

What are the possible outcomes of the event?

· Sprint Backlog and Sprint Goal to be achieved by end of Sprint.
· Developers identify the plan on how to execute the work.
· Scrum Team has transparency on objective and plan for the Sprint.

Daily Scrum

Timebox

Timebox length for a 1-month Sprint? Does it change for shorter Sprints?

• 15 minutes, every day.
• Timebox does not change if the duration of the Sprint changes.

Empiricism

How does this event support inspection and adaption and increase transparency?

• Developers inspect the progress towards the Sprint Goal and adapt the Sprint Backlog as needed.
• Transparency is created by inspecting progress on Sprint Backlog items and raising impediments.

Purpose

Why do we do this? What do we get out of it?

The purpose of the Daily Scrum is to inspect the progress towards the Sprint Goal and adapt the plan for the Sprint to achieve it. The Daily Scrum increases transparency between team members and increases the probability of achieving the goal by the end of the Sprint.

Scrum Master

What's their role at this event?

• Ensure the meeting takes place and that everyone understands its purpose and their role in it.
• May facilitate the event if needed so that its goal can be achieved.
• Coach the Developers on how to select the WHAT and organize the HOW.

Product Owner

What's their role at this event?

May observe to get context on progress or help answer questions.

Developers

What's their role at this event?

Developers conduct the Daily Scrum, inspect progress on the work they have selected for the Sprint, and adapt the Sprint Backlog with changes to the plan needed to achieve the Sprint Goal. They also identify impediments and discuss how best to address them.

Inputs

What are the inputs to this event?

Sprint Goal, Sprint Backlog, Definition of Done, charts depicting progress during the Sprint (e.g. burn-down), impediments tracked

Outcomes

What are the possible outcomes of the event?

Updated Sprint Backlog, including updated plan on how to execute the work for the day. Any new impediment that needs resolution is identified.

Sprint Review

Timebox

Timebox length for a 1-month Sprint? Does it change for shorter Sprints?

Up to 4 hours for 1-month Sprints, usually shorter for shorter Sprints

Empiricism

How does this event support inspection and adaption and increase transparency?

The stakeholders inspect what was accomplished during the Sprint and provide feedback to Scrum Team. The Product Backlog and release plans are adapted based on the results of the discussion. This increases transparency.

Purpose

Why do we do this? What do we get out of it?

To get feedback from stakeholders, validate the Increment, and provide transparency on status. The purpose is to adapt the Product Backlog to reflect what the team learned, optimize the value delivered in the next Sprint, and decide whether to release.

Scrum Master

What's their role at this event?

• Ensure the meeting takes place and that everyone understands its purpose and their role in it.
• Facilitate the event if needed so that its goal can be achieved.

Product Owner

What's their role at this event?

• Present the Sprint Goal and the high-level work accomplished in the Sprint.
• Provide status and updates on the release plan.
• Collect feedback from stakeholders and update the Product Backlog as needed.

Developers

What's their role at this event?

• Present the work performed during the Sprint including the PBIs selected in the Sprint Backlog.
• Allow stakeholders to test and validate the Increment produced, and to provide feedback.
• Support the Product Owner in discussions regarding release plans.

Inputs

What are the inputs to this event?

Increment, Sprint Backlog and Sprint Goal, previous Increments, Product Backlog, Product Goal, Vision, release plan.

Outcomes

What are the possible outcomes of the event?

• Updated Product Backlog and priorities
• Decision to release or not release yet the product.
• Updated Release plan.
• Decision to stop any further development of the product.
• Updates to the Product Goal.
• Status updates to stakeholders.

Sprint Retrospective

Timebox

Timebox length for a 1-month Sprint? Does it change for shorter Sprints?

Up to 3 hours for 1-month Sprints, usually shorter for shorter Sprints

Empiricism

How does this event support inspection and adaption and increase transparency?

The Scrum Team inspects how it is doing the work, its processes, and its performance. Identifies opportunities for improvement. Creates transparency on what works well and what can be improved.

Purpose

Why do we do this? What do we get out of it?

Support continuous improvement for the Scrum Team on processes, performance, and team happiness. Reinforce what works well and identify opportunities for improvement. Identify action items for improvement to work on in the next Sprints.

Scrum Master

What's their role at this event?

• Ensure the meeting takes place and that everyone understands its purpose and their role in it.
• Facilitate the event if needed so that its goal can be achieved.
• Participate as team member in the Scrum Team.

Product Owner

What's their role at this event?

• Participate as a member of the Scrum Team.
• Identify opportunities for improvement for the Scrum Team.

Developers

What's their role at this event?

• Participate as a member of the Scrum Team.
• Identify opportunities for improvement for the Scrum Team.

Inputs

What are the inputs to this event?

Performance of the team during the Sprint, impediments, quality measures of the work performed.

Outcomes

What are the possible outcomes of the event?

One or more opportunities for improvement for the Scrum Team to be addressed as soon as possible (action items).
Updated Definition of Done.

INTERVIEW WITH JEFF SUTHERLAND

CO-FOUNDER OF SCRUM

Jeff Sutherland co-founded Scrum and presented it to the world at the OOPSLA conference in 1995 together with Ken Schwaber. We sat down with Jeff to talk about the origins of Scrum and how he grew it to become the most widely adopted Agile framework. In this conversation, Jeff also shares tips on how to make Scrum teams become highly productive.

Scrum has changed the world of work. Looking back, did you ever imagine that it would have this impact?

Jeff Sutherland: There were 10 years of prototyping Scrum between 1983 and1993, when the first Scrum team was formed. Then of course, in 1995, I got together with Ken Schwaber and we started promoting Scrum to the world. But in 1993, when we created the first Scrum team, I had done many startups and I knew that technology had to be 10 times better in order to get acceptance. We benchmarked. We took the best technology in the world from Capers Jones's company, Software Productivity Research, and we measured the performance of the team. Only when it was 10 times better in terms of both speed and quality, did we say, "Okay, we have something that really works."

And then, the Agile Manifesto happened. That was a major turning point in terms of publicity for Agile practices. At the time, we had more teams doing extreme programming than doing Scrum. In fact, those were the only two major methodologies that were deployed with hundreds of teams. But, as soon as the Agile Manifesto started and Scrum started to expand, what people found was, first of all, that Scrum works anywhere, not just with software technologies. Second, it is really easy to implement. You could put it up in a couple of days. Third, it scales in a way that extreme programming does not. By design, it will support many teams and it is extremely effective when working remotely. Those four factors started to expand the deployment of Scrum to the point where within a few years, we had a 70%, 80% market share which we continue to have today.

You can never tell what is going to happen, but you try to set it up in the right way, and then you can take advantage of the opportunity when the market really opens up as it did with the Agile Manifesto.

Scrum is a massive research project. In fact, recently, the Gartner Group asked me to indicate where all of the pieces of Scrum came from. I went back to 1983. Even in that prototype, we had burndown charts. We had Sprint Planning. We had small teams.

Then, in the rollout, the large companies that implemented Scrum, tested it on thousands and thousands of teams and we reviewed all of the feedback. Ken and I regularly update the Scrum Guide to try to keep it in tune with what people need. It has been a massive effort.

Over the years of course, with your company, but also with the other organizations that you and Ken have been part of, you have been able to work with trainers, consultants, and coaches around the world and collected additional feedback and scaled all of that input, right?

Jeff S.: Right. What we have learned in the last few years, is that in order for teams to perform and to be effective, at companies like Toyota, the Scrum Guide is just the beginning. We have to make sure that the basic Lean tools and techniques are implemented. Scrum derives from Lean. We have to make sure that the high productive patterns in the patterns book that we spent 10 years writing, are implemented, or else you cannot achieve high performance rates.

Finally, we need to be able to scale teams without slowing down as you add more teams. We know how to do that at the enterprise level. Most scaling frameworks are just for the IT group, right? No, we need the whole enterprise, and we need to scale it to thousands of teams. The productivity for the first team cannot slow down when we have 3,000 teams like Amazon has.

You often say twice the work in half the time. What is one key ingredient that will actually be able to achieve that?

Jeff S.: Well, there are at least a dozen items that are essential to have. First, you must have small teams. The optimal team size is 4 to 5 people. You can test that for yourself. In the patterns book, we say that as soon as you get to 7 people, there will be a noticeable slowdown and you need to start to split up. That is because of communication overhead.

Second, there is the backlog that the team brings into the Sprint. We have multiple research studies published in the IEEE [Institute of Electrical and Electronics Engineers] digital library showing that a really good backlog doubles the speed of the team.

You could go twice as fast just by cleaning up your backlog (e.g., just by removing features that are not focused on the goal). You could go twice as fast by cutting the team size from 10 or 15 down to 5. You can go twice as fast by implementing a pattern we call the *Interrupt Buffer*. Teams are interrupted, so you need a way to manage the interrupts. If you do that properly, that could double the team's production.

That is because now you can focus on the work and also manage any unexpected work against your way without being interrupted.

Jeff S.: There is a pattern called Swarming. We actually spent 5 years in the Scrum Pattern Group coming to an agreement on *Swarming* and getting people working together on the same stories. An Indian team that I was working with, was asking me, "What metric should we measure for our Scrum teams? What should our KPIs [Key Performance Indicators] be?"

I said that the only one that matters is process efficiency. Process efficiency is the primary metric at Toyota. It is the actual work time divided by the clock time. So, if you have a story that should take half a day and it takes 2 weeks to get it done, then half a day divided by 10 working days is 5%. That team will be really slow. If you move that process efficiency over 50%, you are guaranteed to double your velocity. So, this Indian team put this metric in the Scrum tooling.

That Indian team started their 2-week Sprint and on the morning of the fourth day, the work was completed. It was really ironic. They called me and said, "We do not know what to do. We do not have any more backlog. We will have to talk to management and ask them what we should do for the rest of the Sprint." So, I asked the team, "How did you get your process efficiency to 80% in 3 days?" And they said, "We put 3 people on every story." So, that is how long it takes. It takes 3 days to implement *Swarming*.

Twice the work in half the time is not that fast. You can do much better than that. I have a guy from Nigeria who had a grant from the Ford Foundation building energy startups, sustainable energy. He came to New York to one of my product owner classes. He said, "Jeff, twice the work in half the time. That is really conservative. I just read your book, and then I did what was in your book. I have 3 companies and they are all doing 3 times the work in a third of the time."

So, 9 times?

Jeff S.: I am not trying to put stress on the team. I am just telling you that it is easy. If you are more productive, you are going to be happier as a team. Your management is going to be happier. Your investors are going to be happier. And your customers are going to be happier. Let us go back to the Agile Manifesto. What is the primary function of the Agile Manifesto? That is putting the customer first and making them happy.

And doing all of that without compromising quality.

Jeff S.: Obviously, they are not happy unless the quality is really high. You want to double the quality. You want to double the speed. Customers are not interested in waiting around. They are not interested in your Scrum team being late. They want it now. The faster you can deliver with quality, the happier the customer is going to be, and the more successful your company is going to be. That is the secret of success.

People should just understand why Toyota became the most successful auto company in the world. Maybe one of the most successful companies in the world. It is because their process efficiency was high. The value delivery was high. The process efficiency reduces the cost, and the value delivery makes the product more valuable.

Why is Tesla now worth four times as much as Toyota? What is the difference?

Because of the value that they deliver?

Jeff S.: That is right. The value that they deliver. You know, in some aspects, their cars are not better than Toyota. They are faster. They are cooler. But the speed of introducing new technology onto the assembly line with the cars rolling out, is 52 times faster than their competitors.

I read recently that somebody disassembled a Tesla and another car. They did that again 3 months later, and noticed that there were way more changes in the Tesla than in the other car.

Jeff S.: That was Sandy Munro's work. That is where I am getting the numbers from. He said that, in one quarter, there were 13 new hardware innovations on the car rolling out of the line, and that some of them are really significant like the heat exchange technology. Most cars have heating/cooling for the engine, if it is electric for the batteries. Then, they have heating/cooling for the interior of the car. They have 3 different systems. Tesla reduced that to 1 system for a third of the cost, a third of the size, and the efficiency is 3 times better.

This is 9 times better than any other manufacturer's heating/ cooling. As a result, Tesla is going to move into the heating/ cooling business in houses, and they are going to disrupt the construction industry because they can replace your air conditioner, your heater, your humidifier, and your air cleaner, with a system that is a third the size, a third the cost, and uses a third of the electricity to run it. That is just revolutionary.

So, if you are working across all of these different organizations and all of these teams, you have noticed that some have been very successful and some are still struggling, right? Maybe at the beginning, they needed help. When you look at those that are struggling, is there a recurring factor, something that they are not doing properly that makes Scrum struggle?

Jeff S.: We have done a lot of research on this in our training, and also with the trainers we are working with all over the world. We must solve the problem whereby 58% of Scrum teams are late, over budget, and with unhappy customers. They claim to be Agile, but they are obviously not. Initially, when we started looking at those numbers from The Standish Group, which is based on over a million projects globally, some people started complaining. "I do not believe that data."

So, is that the fault of Scrum that it does not work?

Jeff S.: There are 21 pieces in the Scrum Guide. So then, at the beginning of the Scrum training, most of our people coming into training are already doing Scrum so we say, "Okay, take your team and take these cards. Put them on the wall and describe your implementation of Scrum. And which one of these cards, which one of these pieces of Scrum, are you doing well? Which ones are not so well? Which ones are you not doing anything at all?"

We found that in about a third of the 21 items in the Scrum Guide, the average team felt that they were doing well. About a third felt they were doing poorly. The last third felt that they were not doing anything at all. So, we learned that the average Scrum team is like driving a car around town with a flat tire, and they were wondering why they are late for the meeting.

So, we know exactly why, and it all boils down to about a dozen reasons. The teams are not small. The backlog is not good. They are not handling interrupts; they have too many interrupts. They do not have stable teams. Somebody is coming in and yanking people off teams. Or, management is running and changing the backlog in the middle of a Sprint.

All these things that we know that disrupt and cause Scrum teams to fail. This is why we have such a high failure rate at Scrum. It has nothing to do with Scrum. It is all Agile processes. They were all equally bad, and it is because people do not do what needs to be done.

This is now translating into Agile transformations. This occurs in virtually every significant company in the world today. I learned this recently, when I was briefing 600 executives from a huge conglomerate that was running 70 companies. They told me that every one of their competitors in 70 different industries is doing an Agile transformation. I was amazed. I never realized it was that massive.

Nobody can afford to not do it.

Jeff S.: In the latest Forbes Insight Study on Agile transformations, 50.3% do not meet management expectations. Why? One of the major reasons is that Scrum teams inside the transformation are not functioning. That is because 58% of Scrum teams are late or over budget with unhappy customers. That makes the transformation fail. This, in my view, is the biggest problem in the land of Agile. Not just Scrum.

It is just like you are at the track with a race car, but you do not know how to drive a race car and you are losing every race. You say, "Well, it must be the car." No. The professional racers know how to drive these cars; and that is why they win.

Thank you so much for sharing your knowledge, your expertise, and all of the stories.

Jeff S.: Thanks for inviting me. I enjoyed talking with you.

LEARN MORE

This is an abridged version of the interview. To listen to the full interview, please visit our website at www.sprintyourwaytoscrum.com

#1

PRIORITY BUGS SHOW UP DURING THE SPRINT AND DISRUPT IT. WHAT SHOULD WE DO?

At times, a priority change or an emergency appears, and your team needs to take care of it immediately. An example of this could be a critical production bug that needs to be fixed because it is negatively impacting the ability of your customers to use your product.

However, the Scrum Team is in the middle of a Sprint and they already have a Sprint Backlog and a Sprint Goal that they are committed to achieving. The additional work that would be required to fix this priority bug would disrupt the work of the Sprint and ultimately penalize the team. What should they do?

The following are some recommendations:

Create a buffer.

If the team is responsible for product bugs - or for other types of responsive work, like operations and customer support - the team may reserve the capacity in any given Sprint to cover unexpected work. The idea of capacity allocation is that you slice the available capacity and reserve a buffer for unplanned work. For example, if your team has a capacity of 50 points per Sprint, you may decide to reserve 20 points for unplanned work (bugs, unexpected requests, operational issues, etc.), and limit your available capacity for the Sprint at 30 points. Therefore, at Sprint Planning, you select a maximum of 30 points of work for the Sprint Backlog, leaving the other 20 points unplanned.

- If unexpected work shows up during the Sprint, and you need to take care of it right away, you can consume the unplanned capacity and the rest of the work in the Sprint Backlog will be unaffected. Therefore, you can still deliver your Sprint Goal, and support the unexpected work.

- If no unexpected work shows up in the Sprint, and if you have completed the work of the Sprint Backlog, you can always reach out to the Product Owner and ask for the next work items that are in the Product Backlog. Capacity does not go wasted; it is used appropriately, as needed.

Say "no".

When a new request shows up – an unexpected bug, a new priority, or something urgent from your boss – your Product Owner can say, "I get it. This is important. However, we have already committed to the work we are doing in this Sprint, so I will add this new work item to the Product Backlog and I will make sure to prioritize it for the next Sprint."

- Saying no is one of the most important things a Product Owner can say when faced with unexpected requests for new work. It is not that you are not going to work on them, it is just that you are not going to disrupt your current Sprint. You will work on these new requests in a future Sprint.

- **Focus** is a key Scrum value. Keeping the focus on the work that you are committed to, and avoiding disruptions that are caused by unexpected requests in the middle of the Sprint, ensures that the team can be productive and that they can deliver quality work.

Restart your Sprint.

In the unusual event that a new priority shows up and you need to take care of it right away, that you do not have reserved capacity for unplanned work, and that it is going to disrupt your Sprint, then you can replan the Sprint with your team.

- Cancel the current Sprint. Any work in progress goes back to the Product Backlog and gets re-prioritized together with the new work requests.

- Create a new Sprint Backlog and a new Sprint Goal, and incorporate the unexpected work item so that it can be properly addressed.

- Sprint cancellations can be frustrating events as they interrupt the work of the team and disrupt their planning, so they should be considered carefully. However, a Sprint can be canceled when its goal becomes obsolete, and the team should replan the Sprint to set up a new goal.

#2

MY PRODUCT BACKLOG IS HUGE. HOW CAN I PRIORITIZE IT?

When the backlog extends indefinitely into the future, it becomes almost impossible to manage. It is hard to get a full view of it so as to properly prioritize the work items. When new requests come in, where do they go? To the bottom of the backlog, waiting indefinitely to rise to the top and to get worked on? Or somewhere in the middle of the backlog, mixed up with a dozen other things you need to do? Or simply interrupt what you are already doing, become a new priority, and then everything else already in the backlog is pushed further down? Any way you look at it, there is no clear solution to be both responsive to new requests, and to work through the old ones.

A very long backlog also creates a sense of never-ending work for both the Product Owner and the rest of the Scrum Team. It does not matter how much work you tackle in one Sprint, or if you are able to increase your velocity. When you look at the backlog, the amount of work remaining is barely affected. And probably, the reason why the product backlog is that long is that – no matter how fast you work – new requests keep coming in and you simply cannot finish them all. The team feels demotivated, grinding, and uninspired. They get the work done out of integrity, but the work does not provide a sense of accomplishment. Moments of celebrations are missing.

In other situations, a long backlog may be the result of just a huge project that needs to be done. There is a level of complexity or just a lot of functionality that needs to be built out and it is all documented in the backlog as a very lengthy list of requirements. Sometimes, the Product Owner and the Scrum Team create this backlog; sometimes it is given to them by some Stakeholders or by the organization. For example, "We need to replace this legacy application with a modern platform; here is the list of all of the functionalities that we need to re-create in the new platform to get rid of the legacy one." Someone spends months documenting all of the features and functionalities of the new system, making sure nothing is missing; that becomes the team's backlog.

How to manage a long backlog? Trim the backlog and consider a set of experiments:

Trim the backlog:

If you have a long backlog, it is very unlikely that you will get to do everything in the next few months. In fact, your backlog probably represents years of hard work. And by the time you are done with most of it, another long list of work items will be added, further extending it into the future. The point is, a long backlog represents a goal that will never be achieved. You may be better-off by trimming the backlog and by discarding part of it. There are many ways to do this, and I will share a couple of techniques that I have found to be effective with teams:

1) Use MoSCoW or another version of the technique to separate the backlog items into different buckets. Work with your Stakeholders and with your team, and ask them to place each backlog item into one of the buckets. They should be really intentional, thinking about which items are valuable right now, and which are less so or maybe would be in the future. Put a threshold on the "Must" bucket to limit the number of items that can go in there, and force the participants to distribute the items across all of the buckets.

When all of the product backlog items have been assigned to a bucket, take the "Must" bucket and save it. This is your new backlog. And then, take the other buckets and discard them. It may seem brutal, but the reality is that even if you just focus on the items in the "Must" bucket, by the time you get all of them done, more requests will have come your way. You may never get to the other buckets anyway, so why bother?

OK, if you feel really emotional about letting them go, save them in a black box 100 miles away, so that they are not in your backlog anymore, but you know you can always get back to them if you ever need to.

2) When I was a Product Owner, I kept a separate backlog of Epics. My team only worked on one or two Epics at a time: we would get them done, and then select the next Epic(s) from the Epic Backlog, break it down into Stories, and execute the work. To manage the Epic Backlog and to preserve my sanity, I had a simple rule: if an Epic had not "moved" in 6 months, I would delete it from the backlog. This helped me keep the backlog to a manageable size (e.g., this is necessary if you are using WSJF to

prioritize it). And I figured that if an Epic had been removed and it was really important for some Stakeholder, they would come asking about it and I could return it to the backlog.

Consider a set of experiments:

A long backlog often represents the work that is defined for a new product or for a new project. This work is interpreted as "all the things we need to do to build the product." If everything listed in the backlog is required, then the backlog represents a requirement document, expressed in a different form, created with up-front planning and with limited validation. You may build it iteratively using Sprints, but the scope of work is all defined up-front. There is no discovery, no validation, and no iteration on the backlog itself. Everything must be done, and you simply choose to execute the work in Sprints.

I always invite the people I work with, to switch their interpretation and instead to think of the backlog as "the possible things we may do to build the product." What this does, is that it shifts the interpretation of a product backlog item from a "requirement" (something that is required, something we must do), to an "experiment." An experiment is something you may consider doing because you think it can be valuable, but you are really not sure if it is. So, you may consider building a small part of a feature, test it with your customers, and then continue building it if it is really valuable. And if it is not, discard it and move on to the next experiment.

This is a mindset shift that is really important for Product Owners on how they manage their backlogs. When this mindset is present, the backlog is no longer a repository of all of the possible things we need to do to the product. Rather, it is a backlog of experiments, things we can do to validate our ideas and if successful, build the functionality that we have validated. This mindset supports customer-centricity and rapid validation, reducing the risk of building the wrong solution and focusing the work of the team on what is really valuable, rather than building it all.

CASE STUDY

Consider this real-life example of a self-driving auto system. The company creates the sensors and the artificial intelligence software for the self-driving system, and sells it to several automakers that install it in their cars. So far, the company has built a version of the product that is able to drive a car autonomously in a limited set of road conditions, and up to 40 miles/hour (64 km/hr). It has partnered with a few automakers to test the system and to provide feedback.

Recently, the automakers have requested that the system becomes fully autonomous and with a top speed of 80 miles/hour (130 km/hr). This will enable the system to drive on highways and everywhere else with absolutely no assistance from the driver.

From the product team's perspective, the development of this product begins with specifying the full list of conditions and behaviors that the system should support, for example, when there is a car in front; when there is no other car; when the road bends; when the road is bumpy; when it rains, snows, or is sunny; when another car passes on the left, and then suddenly cuts in front; or when a human, an animal, or another small vehicle crosses the street in front of the vehicle.

The list becomes long quite rapidly, as you think of everything that can happen while you are driving, and it grows exponentially large as you consider driving at high speed. This system needs to satisfy all of these conditions; otherwise, the automakers will not be able to safely install it on cars. It is even more complex because we humans have the ability to adapt to new or unexpected situations and to quickly decide how to handle them based on our training, experience, and abilities. A computer algorithm needs clear instructions on how to process a situation and the number of possible combinations in real-life driving scenarios can be infinite. Therefore, the system needs to develop a sophisticated level of artificial intelligence using a number of known patterns and behaviors, and from there, develop the ability to make decisions in situations that do not match a previously known set of criteria.

The backlog becomes impossibly long. And the product team is struggling to make sense of all of it, and to decide where to start from. They face years of work ahead of them before they can even have something that automakers can test.

I helped the team approach the work from a different point of view. Rather than making a list of all possible use cases and conditions and then building them, what if they could identify one use case that is simple and valuable, build it, and validate it with their customers? Based on what they learn, they could then decide what the next use case should be and continue building incrementally.

The team chose as a starting use case the ability for a car to self-drive on a highway with no other cars or obstacles on the course, during a sunny day in full daylight, cruising at speeds of up to 80 miles/hour (130 km/hr) and with no changes in lane. Even in its simplicity, solving this use case was not trivial and required the development of a strong foundation for the system to work at that speed. The question the team wanted to answer was: "Can we build this, and how do we build it?"

The team understood that it was premature to release the product in the market. But, that was not the point. The goal was to build a system that could satisfy a basic use case – in fact, the easiest and most controllable of all – and demonstrate the technologies needed to satisfy it. Learn from it, and then work on the next use case (e.g., drive on a highway and add other cars, or drive on a highway with weather conditions that are not perfect). Validate each use case in the fastest way possible, evaluate the performance of the system, get feedback from the customers, and then add the next use case.

This way of breaking down the backlog into a series of experiments for rapid validation of both technology and real-life application, helped the team get feedback from their customers much sooner than would have been otherwise possible if they had built "the whole thing,", and helped the team strongly improve their productivity.

REFERENCES

1. "Deliver Great Products that Customers Love", by Valerio Zanini 2018— https://www.5dvision.com/books/deliver-great-products-that-customers-love/

#3

MY DEVELOPERS DO NOT PROVIDE ACCURATE ESTIMATES, HENCE, I AM UNABLE TO PROVIDE TIMELINES TO THE CLIENT. HOW CAN I ENCOURAGE THEM TO GIVE ACCURATE ESTIMATES ?

Product Owners depend on Developers to get estimates and project out the timeline of the work. Often, these estimates are not accurate, and the projections are off, creating irritation with the Stakeholders for unmet deadlines. When we look at it, the problem may not be with estimates, but rather with how estimates are used.

Let us consider a few cases:

– Estimates are supposed to be estimates, not precise measurements. While accuracy in estimates is developed over time as the team gets better at understanding the work to be done and its complexity, estimates should never be considered a measure of truth. When it is time to actually do the work, the team may find unexpected complexities, a dependency that was not accounted for, a drop in capacity due to a particular team member not being present, or requests for unexpected work that force the team to change focus and to delay its plan. Any of these throw away any accuracy in estimates. And that is OK. The point is not to learn to make even more accurate estimates or to force the team to stick to them. The point of estimates is to provide a reasonable understanding of the size and complexity of the work so that you can make plans, and then create the transparency needed to update the plans as things change.

– I think it is a myth that people are effective at providing exact estimates. We are good with *guesstimates*! Instead of pushing Developers to provide accurate estimates, as Scrum Masters, we can suggest a few techniques such as Relative Estimation, Affinity Estimation, or Planning Poker. These techniques take the focus away from accuracy in estimates, and instead, create alignment between team members. What matters, is not that estimates are accurate; rather it is important that they are reliable, with a level of consistency. This is developed over time as the Developers learn more about the work they are doing, and how to make estimates.

– Establish slack in the system. Rather than loading your Sprints to capacity, create an *Interrupt Buffer* [1] and load the Sprint below your team's capacity. This allows you to compensate for any "wrong" estimate, in case the actual work is larger than expected. It also allows the team to adapt to unexpected events (someone gets sick, or the company holds an all-hands meeting). Having a buffer in your capacity planning is considered one of the most effective ways to help teams deliver on their commitments and to increase productivity.

– The 4th Agile value states that we value more, "responding to change over following a plan." Plans are useful and important – we would not be able to do much without a plan – and we recognize that plans are not set in stone. When things change – as they always do – when we learn more about the work that we need to do, when things happen that make the plan look unrealistic, we should be able to update the plan and to respond to the change. And this value should inform the mindset of Stakeholders too, since they should understand that any plan that we put together, is going to change and that they should work with us to update the plan and be aligned. In fact, transparency about the plan and any changes to it, is critical for the successful relationship between the Scrum Team and its Stakeholders. And this applies to timelines too (a part of a plan) so that when they change, the Stakeholders are part of the decision-making process.

– When projected timelines change and differ from what you had planned, the Product Owner can work with Stakeholders on three dimensions:

1) **Time:** Based on the progress of the work and the current velocity, the Product Owner projects that to complete the work, it will take longer than expected. The question then becomes, can we extend the timeline? For example, we promised the Stakeholders to deliver the next release by June, and right now it looks like we will not be done until mid-July. Is this still OK? The Stakeholders may understand where the Product Owner is coming from, the complexity of the work, and the causes for the delay, and accept the new timeline. They also understand that this may change and that at the moment that is our best projection based on the information that we have available. Alternatively, the Stakeholders may not accept the extension. They may say: "You promised June, and we communicated it to the Board that we would have a release in June, so June needs to be it." In this case, "time" cannot be extended, and we now look at the second dimension, scope.

2) **Scope:** When the Product Owner projects that the work will take longer than expected, but the timeline is fixed, the second option is to work on scope. You look at all of the work remaining to be done before the deadline, and you reprioritize it and decide what needs to be completed by the deadline and what can be dropped. The conversation with the Stakeholders goes like this: "I have shown you that the team's velocity is slower than expected and that we will not be able to complete all of the work by the deadline. I fully understand that the timeline is fixed. The second option we have is to look at the scope of work. Are there things that are more important than others, and are there things we can remove from the plan in order to meet the deadline?" The Product Owner can then work with the Stakeholders to reprioritize the backlog and to decide which work items can be dropped from the plan. Alternatively, the Stakeholders may not accept the change of scope. They may say: "You promised June, and you promised the entire scope." In this case, you are left with the third option, capacity.

3) **Capacity:** When the deadline is fixed and the scope of work is also fixed, you can only work on the third dimension, capacity. If you were able to accelerate delivery of the work, you could

finish all of the promised work by the deadline. The trick is, how do you accelerate? You need to increase the capacity for your team. Basically, you need additional people, maybe even an extra team.

By working with Stakeholders across the three dimensions, you create transparency and empower them to make the right choice to support you and to achieve what they need.

REFERENCES

1. Scrum Pattern Group https://www.scrumplop.org/

#4

PRODUCT OWNERS AND DEVELOPERS FEEL THAT THEY ARE SPENDING TOO MUCH TIME CREATING AND REFINING STORIES, YET THE REQUIREMENTS ARE UNCLEAR. WHAT SHOULD WE DO ?

The team spends too much time refining the stories and adding every conceivable detail. They complain that the requirements are unclear, and this seems to be a never-ending circle of blame. Why? Let us look at a few possible situations and what you can do to tackle them.

– **Fear of commitment and failure.** The team feels they cannot commit if they do not know all of the details. They see commitment as an obstacle and are afraid of it. Are there penalties when the team does not complete the work? Is there blame? Is empowerment present? A possible way to tackle this is to establish a buffer on capacity. This removes the pressure from having all of the details understood and leaves room for the Developers to complete the work.

– **The team is used to taking marching orders from the Product Owner.** They execute the work that someone has given them, and therefore, they need all of the details specified up-front. There is no collaboration on defining the details, and no collaboration during the Sprint in clarifying details and in making decisions. This may create the expectation that the work done at the end of the Sprint cannot be modified (i.e., we need to get it right) with no opportunity for experimentation or for iteration. Work is really planned up-front and executed in chunks.

– **The team should review the relationship between the Product Owner and the Developers.** The two roles belong to the Scrum Team. They work together all the time, during the Sprint. They have different responsibilities. The Product Owner may feel the pressure of giving the team all of the answers. In reality, the Product Owner has the responsibility of giving the team the "problem" to solve, and the context around it – "why this is important and why customers care." The solution should come from the Developers. Whether the details of the solution are defined earlier or during the Sprint, the responsibility remains with the Developers. To make this work, it is important to foster transparency and collaboration between both the Product Owner and the Developers.

– **Teams often compensate with the addition of a Business Analyst (BA)** someone dedicated to write all of the requirements and to refine the stories. While each situation is different, the role of the BA should not be a cover-up for a lack of collaboration and empowerment of the Product Owner-Developers relationship. The strength of the team will grow if this relationship is strengthened.

LEARN MORE

Refinement of the Product Backlog is a continuous activity for the Product Owner – ideally they do this every day by adding work items to the backlog, removing those that are no longer needed, adding details to some, and splitting others that may be too big. This is to say that there is no hard and set rule for how much time you should spend in refining the backlog. However, if you find yourself spending too much time writing User Stories, adding all of the details and acceptance criteria, and making sure all of the requirements are properly identified, maybe there is something to look at. Are you using User Stories for what they were designed, or just as a substitute for requirements?

Let us look at how User Stories can be used to foster a deeper collaboration between the Product Owner and the Developers.

The User Story format is just - like the name implies – a format. Its purpose is not to write a list of requirements in a different way. Rather, the purpose of the User Story format is to change the paradigm of the interaction between the Product Owner and Developers. Let us explain.

Without User Stories, a Product Owner would write a list of requirements, and then pass these on to the Developers. They would have questions, and the Product Owner would add more specifics to the requirements. When these are detailed enough that the Developers know exactly what is expected of them, the Product Owner can confirm the requirements to the Developers for implementation.

User Stories change this dynamic. The goal of a User Story is to clarify the respective responsibilities of the Product Owner (responsible for what and why) and the Developers (responsible for how) on a Scrum Team, foster collaboration, and leverage the expertise of the whole team to find the best solution.

Rather than defining all possible requirements or providing a complete understanding to the Developers so that they can execute the request, a User Story provides just enough context around the work you need to do as a team, and then opens up the conversation about what is the best solution you can devise together.

The User Story provides the context around who the user is, what they need, and why they need it. Rather than giving all of the requirements, the details of the solution emerge from the conversation. The Developers, in collaboration with the Product Owner, define the details, the acceptance criteria, the technical specs, the performance requirements, and how the solution is going to provide what the user is looking for. By collaborating with the Developers, User Stories shift the responsibility of identifying all of the requirements from the Product Owner to the Scrum Team as a whole. And from this collaboration stems the possibility to create better solutions for the end users whose needs you are trying to solve.

So, if you find yourself spending too much time writing User Stories, reflect on how you can stop doing it and get help from your Developers. How can you make this a collaborative activity rather than a top-down directive?

5

IS IT OK FOR MY DEVELOPERS TO DIRECTLY SPEAK WITH THE CUSTOMERS, OR SHOULD I BE THE IN-BETWEEN GO-TO PERSON ?

Ever played the "Telephone Game"? It is that game where someone whispers a sentence in another person's ear, and this person in turns whispers a sentence in the next person's ear, and so on until the last person receives the message. In a typical instance of the game, the sentence received by the last person is often different, reinterpreted, or completely transformed from the initial one. The Telephone Game happens when the Product Owner is the one interfacing with the Stakeholders and with the customers, collecting all of the requirements and needs, and then translating them to the Developers who never get to leave their black box. The Developers get their marching orders and are asked to build a solution. For them, the Product Owner is a proxy, and the Developers have no direct experience of what the customers really need.

– This setup is very limiting for the Developers, can be very cumbersome for the Product Owner, and frequently leads to botched product decisions based on one person's understanding of the problem (based on what the Product Owner shares) or on the interpretation of the requirements by the team.

– Compare this setup to a different one where the Product Owner invites the Developers to directly experience the customers' needs and to develop a direct understanding of the business context in which they operate. The Developers can then understand the problem that customers are trying to solve, and the market in which the company operates. From this understanding, the Developers may be able to provide fresh ideas, offer new perspectives, and collaborate with the Product Owner on problem solving.

– This does not mean that the Product Owner abdicates their responsibilities. They remain the only one responsible for understanding Stakeholders and customers' needs, and for priority decisions on the product. The Product Owner simply offers the rest of the team an opportunity to have a deeper perspective on the work they are doing.

– We invite Product Owners to connect the Developers to the Stakeholders and to the customers. This provides an enormous context and understanding for the Developers, rather than relying on the Product Owner to act as a proxy. One way to do this is to invite the Developers – maybe one at a time on a rotational basis – to join the Product Owner in customer discovery activities, such as interviews or usability testing.

REAL STORY

When I was at Capital One, I made a point of going out of the office every Thursday to visit our local branches, to talk to bankers, and to interview customers. This gave me a deeper perspective on the needs and problems that bankers and customers were facing, and it also provided me with the possibility of getting rapid feedback on any ideas I had.

I made a point of bringing with me one Developer from my team when I went for interviews. We did this on a rotational basis, so that every Developer on the team got an opportunity to talk with customers every once in a while.

The end result was that my team developed a deeper understanding of the space in which we operated, and was able to contribute ideas to our product – sometimes ideas that were much better than the ones I could come up with.

#6

MY CEO WANTS TO CHANGE THE PRIORITIES IN THE MIDDLE OF THE SPRINT. WHAT SHOULD I DO ?

If the CEO – or a customer, or anyone else in the company – has an urgent need for a new priority, the correct course of action is to go to the Product Owner and to discuss with them the new priority. Most likely, the Scrum Team is somewhere in the middle of a Sprint and – except for rare and super-urgent instances – the Product Owner decides not to interrupt the Sprint, but rather to prioritize the work for a future Sprint.

– In Scrum, the Product Backlog is the single source of work for the Scrum Team. It means that if an item is not in the Product Backlog, the team should not work on it. This creates empowerment for the Product Owner, and gives them the responsibility to decide what work gets prioritized for the team, and what needs to wait.

– The Sprint Backlog represents the commitment that the Developers have taken for the current Sprint, represented by the list of work items selected to be completed in the Sprint. It is important to empower the Developers to own their Sprint Backlog and to avoid changing priorities or affecting it. Any such change negatively affects the ability of the team to deliver on their commitment and to achieve the Sprint Goal.

– If new priorities often show up in the middle of a Sprint, consider implementing an *Interrupt Buffer*[1, 2]: Reserve part of your capacity in a given Sprint for unplanned work. If a new priority shows up, you can use the buffer to deal with it, rather than disrupting the work already in the Sprint Backlog.

REFERENCES

1. Teams that Finish Early Accelerate Faster: A Pattern Language for High Performing Scrum Teams https://www.scruminc.com/wp-content/uploads/2014/05/teamsthatfinishearlyacceleratefaster.pdf
2. Scrum Pattern Group https://www.scrumplop.org/

#7

I HAVE MULTIPLE STAKEHOLDERS: HOW DO I PRIORITIZE THEIR DIFFERENT NEEDS?

Needs can come from different users of your product, or from different internal stakeholders who sometimes may conflict with each other. For example, one stakeholder may want you to incorporate in your product the ability to snap photos and post them on social media. Another stakeholder may want an Artificial Intelligence (AI) system that is able to understand human language and perform tasks as directed.

As a Product Owner, you know that you will not be able to satisfy all of these needs at once. There are different ways to prioritize the needs and one that I like to use is the **Problem-Opportunity Scoring Model**[1]. I like this model because it grounds the decision on a deeper understanding of the problem each stakeholder is trying to solve, providing for better context in making a decision.

Start by understanding each need in detail, especially the problem that your user or stakeholder is trying to solve (I find it useful to write these as problem statements focusing on the context, the user, the problem, and the impact to the user). Then, define a few dimensions that make sense for you and that can help quantify each need. For example, you may consider the following dimensions:

- **Severity** = How severe is the problem when users experience it?

- **Frequency** = How frequently does the problem occur?

- **Population size** = Are there few or many people experiencing it?

- **Value** = What is the value to the customers and/or to the business if we solve this?

- **Opportunity** = Does solving this need create a greater opportunity for the business?

Next, estimate these dimensions for each of the needs you have in your list. Assign a score of 1 to 10 to each dimension; 10 being the highest. Use relative estimation to compare different needs, and you do not need to use all of the values (e.g., different needs may score "2" for the same dimension).

Once you have scored each need across the dimensions, you can add the values and rank the needs from highest to lowest. This gives you a sense of the priorities and which need to solve first.

Problem-Opportunity Scoring Model

Need	Severity	Frequency	Population size	Value	Opportunity	Rank

Assign a score 1 to 10 to each dimension, 10 being highest

REFERENCES

1. Problem-Opportunity Scoring Model—https://www.5dvision.com/post/problem-opportunity-scoring-model/

#8

CAN WE USE THE SPRINT REVIEW TO DO REFINEMENT ?

The purpose of the Sprint Review is to inspect the Increment produced by the Scrum Team during the Sprint, collect feedback from the Stakeholders, and adapt the Product Backlog to reflect the input received from the Stakeholders. This should be a working session where the Scrum Team and the Stakeholders collaborate in reviewing the Increment and in deciding what to do next.

The Sprint Review is not the right time to do refinement. However, it is useful to inspect the Product Backlog and discuss with the Stakeholders whether the next priorities are indeed valuable, or there is something else more important to work on in the future Sprints.

The participants can review the Product Backlog to align on what work to do next. Decisions should be reflected in changes to the Product Backlog and may include new priorities, new features that get added to the Product Backlog, and additional details to an already planned work item. In this sense, the Product Backlog gets inspected and adapted during the Sprint Review as a collaboration with the Stakeholders.

However, this is not the right time to spend on nitty-gritty details, requirements, splitting down User Stories, or estimates. A separate refinement session within the Scrum Team can be used for this.

#9

WE HAVE DISENGAGED STAKEHOLDERS. HOW OFTEN SHOULD THE PRODUCT OWNER BE MEETING WITH THEM AND HOW SHOULD WE KEEP THEM ENGAGED ?

As the Product Owner, you are responsible for Stakeholder management. Stakeholders represent anyone who has a stake, or an interest, in your product, including customers, end users, managers, and partners. You should know and fully understand their concerns, needs, and problems-to-solve. You should understand what they value in your product or in your product ideas, and how your product is going to address their needs. When you do this, it is no longer a problem of how often you meet with them, but how you leverage your relationship with them to make informed decisions about the product you are building and to create transparency about these decisions.

Managing a large group of Stakeholders can be a daunting task, especially for Product Owners who are already busy with so many other activities. So how to best manage Stakeholders? Let us offer a few tips:

Leverage Sprint Reviews

The Sprint Review takes place at the end of every Sprint. Are your Stakeholders participating?

Make the Sprint Review valuable for your Stakeholders. Use the time wisely. For example, they may not be fully interested in seeing the latest iteration of your new database. Instead, they may contribute valuable input to the steps in the product development.

Consider the fact that the Sprint Review is more than just a demo. The purpose of the Sprint Review is for the Stakeholders to inspect the Increment, to provide feedback on the work that got completed, and to collaborate on what to do next. This last part is important. It means that the Sprint Review is an opportunity to share the Roadmap, the Product Backlog, the Release Plan, and the priorities, and then to collaborate with the Stakeholders on what is important and what to do next. Rather than just as a demo, you can use the Sprint Review as a collaborative working session with your Stakeholders.

Tips for effective Sprint Reviews:

- Coach the Stakeholders explaining the purpose of the Sprint Review. Highlight how their feedback and their guidance will be of benefit to the business (something they care about).

- If they skip the Sprint Review, share with them the link to the demonstration or to a recording if possible (maximum: a 15-min clip) and follow up for feedback.

- If any of their feedback was implemented and was being demonstrated in the upcoming Sprint Review meeting, make sure that it is highlighted and that you tell them.

- Share the next priorities in the Product Backlog and where you are in the Roadmap or in the Release Plan, and ask for their feedback on what is most valuable to do next. Are these the right priorities?

- In the next Sprint, as soon as the Sprint Planning is over, share a 2-page "Sprint Overview" informing them about the Sprint Goal, the list of User Stories forecasted, and other important information that will add value. This will set the expectation for the next Sprint Review.

- If there are major changes or impediments during the Sprint which may impact the Sprint Goal, keep them informed and ask for help in solving impediments.

Decide who the key Stakeholders are

You may have a long list of Stakeholders, but not all of them are equally important in the success of your product. For example, a customer may have an interest in your product that is solving a key problem they are facing. A manager may just be there to check that you do your job properly. One Stakeholder may give you insights on what value your product is delivering, and on what areas you should then concentrate on. The other Stakeholders may just offer guidance or maybe alignment to the company's mission. Depending on your product's journey, you may need more input from just one Stakeholder. And this may change at later stages of your product development.

The point is, identify who the key Stakeholders are and whose input, feedback, and insights can help you make the right decisions regarding the product. Work with them more closely, and keep the others informed.

Facilitate group workshops

An effective way of working with Stakeholders and avoiding getting trapped into one-on-one negotiations, is to get all of the key Stakeholders in a room together and to facilitate a conversation around the topic at the end. Let them share their different opinions, give a voice to all of their concerns and perspectives, and then come to a decision.

An example of this is in the early stages of product development, during the Design phase, when you craft a Product Vision. I find it very effective to do this collaboratively with the key Stakeholders, using the Product Vision Canvas[1] as a framework to facilitate the conversation around the different components that are important for a Product Vision. This creates alignment and enrollment into the vision for your product.

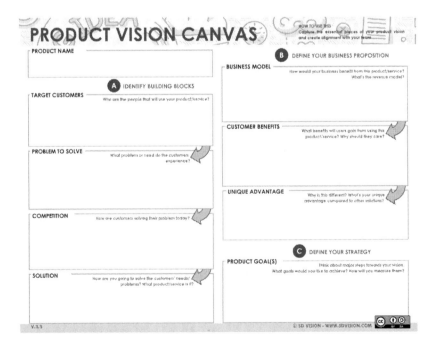

Act as a Product Owner

Often, I see Product Owners request permission from various Stakeholders to work on a new feature, to change their Roadmap, or to give space to the team to solve a technical debt that is negatively impacting the performance of the product. These Product Owners often wait for approval before taking action. While there is nothing wrong in getting insights from Stakeholders or in creating transparency about the decisions you are making, if you want to become a Product Owner, you have to stop acting as an order taker, and instead assume ownership. This sometimes means saying no to some Stakeholders when their request does not fit within your vision, priorities, or simply the current plan. Sometimes, it means changing the way in which you present yourself, or how you present your product plan. Show ownership, create transparency, and keep everyone informed of the steps you are taking. Own it.

REFERENCES

1. Product Vision Canvas—https://www.5dvision.com/agile-product-frameworks/product-vision-canvas/

#10

I AM MANAGING TWO IMPORTANT PRODUCTS. HOW CAN I PRIORITIZE THE WORK BETWEEN THE TWO ?

Here are a few tips on how to deal with this:

– Break down the work in smaller chunks so that it becomes easier to mix different categories of work.

– Understand where each product stands in the lifecycle. For instance, for a mature product you may do maintenance work, and for a "horizon 2" product, you may need to do some early-stage validation. In the market, one is a cash cow; the other represents the future of your company. Having this understanding may help you decide where to focus, or how to divide your time between the two products.

- Use capacity allocation to reserve capacity for each product (e.g., 60% of capacity for product A, 30% of capacity for product B, and the remaining 10% as a buffer). This creates clear boundaries and allows you to move the two products forward concurrently.

#11

WHAT HAPPENS TO THE TEAM LEAD/TECH LEAD ROLE WHEN WE USE SCRUM; IS IT OK FOR THEM TO ACT AS EITHER THE PRODUCT OWNER OR AS THE SCRUM MASTER?

The Team Lead is typically in a positional authority compared to the Developers. The same can be said of a Manager. This can create some unwanted dynamics within the team, preventing it from really being self-managing and causing downward pressure on the Developers. Scrum expects the Scrum Team to be self-organizing and self-managing, but does not provide specific guidance about the Team Lead role.

In my experience, I have seen the following scenarios:

– Team Leads become Product Owners or Scrum Masters and they perform those responsibilities. When they do, it's important that they renounce any positional authority on the rest of the team, and become peers. If the Manager or the Team Lead is also the Product Owner for the team, they tend to command the team and this is not what the Product Owner should do. In fact, the Product Owner should be a peer to the Developers, with a different set of responsibilities.

– Team Leads remove themselves from the actual work and align to the overall Agile transformation plan as servant leaders. They provide their support to the Scrum Teams by mentoring them, by helping them identify which Agile frameworks are best suited, by assisting them in forming cross-functional and self-managing teams, and so forth.

REAL STORY

A software development team in a large U.S. bank was building a critical security application for the bank. They had already spent months working on this application, with only limited results. The team was struggling to complete the work, and the Stakeholders were frustrated by the lack of progress.

During one Sprint Planning meeting, I observed the Product Owner assign 60 points of work to the team. The team took the marching orders and committed to the Sprint Backlog as was given to them.

When the Sprint ended, I checked again with the team and they had completed only 27 points. This was less than 50% of their initial commitment. It bothered me, so I started digging into the historical performance of the team, looking at the burn-down charts of previous Sprints. And I discovered that this team was always committed to 60 points and had never been able to complete more than 27 points. The overcommitment left them frustrated, unempowered, and dealing with a ton of multitasking that slowed things down even further.

When I asked the team why they committed to 60 points when their velocity was not even half of that, they said: "Because the Product Owner is our manager."

I then went to the manager, and asked why he gave 60 points of work to the team even if they had never shown that they were able to complete more than 27 points. And he said: "This is my team, and I decide how much work they should do. Besides, if I give them less than that, they start slacking."

It took a bit of negotiation, but at the end, I was able to convince the manager to run an experiment at the following Sprint. We agreed to give work to the team based on their capacity. So, the team was given 27 points, and by the end of the Sprint they delivered 30 points. This was miraculous, as the team had never been able to go above 27 points before.

Armed with the result, I asked the Product Owner/manager to run another experiment, again limiting the work to the team's capacity. And for the second Sprint, the team delivered 33 points. Compared to where they started, 33 points completed in a Sprint represented a 20% increase in performance for the team. Even the manager was surprised by the result, and agreed to let the team work at capacity for subsequent Sprints, rather than imposing the work top-down.

Later, I spoke with leadership and we decided that it was in the best interest of the team to get a new Product Owner who had no direct authority over the team. So, the company hired an outsider who joined the team as a peer.

#12

SHOULD THE PRODUCT OWNER BE PRESENT IN ALL REFINEMENT MEETINGS ?

The short answer is yes, because the Product Owner provides the context needed in order for refinement to be successful. Refinement of the Product Backlog is a continuous activity for the Product Owner - ideally, they do this every day by adding work items to the backlog, by removing those that are no longer needed, by adding details to some, and by splitting others that may be too cumbersome. It is an ongoing activity throughout the Sprint and the goal is to get the work items ready for a future Sprint.

However, it is useful for the Product Owner to hold regular refinement meetings with Developers and with a few Subject

Matter Experts (SMEs), as needed. This provides an opportunity for everyone to learn about the content of the Product Backlog, its priorities, and what to expect in upcoming Sprints. And it also allows the Product Owner to get additional information from the Developers, for example, about estimates.

– Many Product Owners conduct Refinement meetings with Stakeholders to get a better understanding of the requirements and to discuss how to maximize the business value of the prioritized items.

– With the Developers, there may be more than one Refinement meeting during the Sprint to prepare work items for an upcoming Sprint. However, it is typically a good practice to limit the amount of time Developers spend in refinement meetings because it is time taken away from doing the work. One way to do this is to invite only one or two Developers to the meeting, rather than the whole team.

– The refinement meeting should not replace the Sprint Planning meeting. Remember, Sprint Planning is used to decide which Stories are selected for a Sprint, and how the work will be implemented. Therefore, refinement meetings should not be used to schedule a Sprint or create a Sprint Backlog. Instead, refinement is intended to provide context about the work for upcoming Sprints (typically the next 2-3 Sprints), to identify dependencies, to provide rough estimates of the work to the Product Owner, and to discuss any external help that may be needed to perform the work (so that the help can be requested ahead of time rather than waiting for the Sprint to start). At Sprint Planning, the team will select the list of work items to complete in the Sprint, and discuss how to organize the work.

EXAMPLE

Team Purple has two Refinement meetings every Sprint – 2 hours each. During the 1st meeting, the Product Owner talks about the possible Goal for the upcoming Sprint and presents the list of prioritized User Stories in the Product Backlog. The Developers review and refine each User Story and get them in a ready state for the upcoming Sprint Planning meeting. The Developers are able to review half of the User Stories; in the 2nd Refinement meeting (conducted after a couple of days) the Developers resume the process of reviewing the remaining User Stories. They identify those that potentially could be selected for the next Sprint, and refine a few more just in case priorities changes.

It is helpful if the Product Owner is attending both of the Refinement meetings because there may be times when the Product Owner has to provide a clarification or shed more light on the requirements. Also, the Product Owner may reprioritize the items if necessary based on the estimates provided by the Developers and by the dependencies being discussed in that meeting. Helping the Developers understand the overall context enables them to make better decisions for upcoming Sprints.

#13

SHOULD THE PRODUCT OWNER BE A PART OF THE RETROSPECTIVE ?

The Retrospective (also called "Retro") is an opportunity to identify improvements for the team, so that over time the Scrum Team can improve its performance, processes, work environment, and team well-being. As such, the Retro is for the whole Scrum team, including the Scrum Master and the Product Owner who participate as peer members of the Scrum team.

If the team has concerns about having the Product Owner participate at the Retro, this is a sign that some strain exists between the Developers and the Product Owner. Rather than leaving it hidden, the relationship between the Product Owner and the Developers should be discussed. Is there positional authority? Is there fear of failure or fear of opening up?

Example: The Product Owner in the client organization, and the Developers in the contractor company. The relationship between the two is one of order giver to order takers, and the Developers feel that they do not want to open up because they are afraid of ruining the relationship with their client. Address this with coaching on roles and responsibilities. Create opportunities for openness and for trust. Make sure everyone understands the impact of this relationship and propose ways to improve.

Here are a few tips:

– Create a safe space

– Clarify roles in the Scrum Team and their responsibilities

– Run a focused Retro on relationships within the team and between the roles

– Run an anonymous Retro when fear is present (you can use an online retrospective tool to anonymize inputs)

– The Retrospective is also time for bonding, for instance, schedule a happy hour as a Retro.

#14

WHAT IS THE
DIFFERENCE BETWEEN
A PRODUCT OWNER
AND A PRODUCT
MANAGER ?

The Product Owner and the Product Manager are roles that are defined within an organization typically to distinguish between a different level of responsibility or seniority. From a competency point of view, the competency is Product Management and it is the same for both roles. From the point of view of the expertise and of the type of work they do, there should be no difference. Both do discovery, ideation, planning, execution, and so forth. However, the two roles differ in their scope and in their focus:

The **Product Owner** is a role on a Scrum Team. The Scrum Guide (2020 edition) defines the Product Owner as the role that is accountable for maximizing the value of the product resulting from the work of the Scrum Team. How this is done, varies across the organization and in general, includes a combination of the following activities:

- Communicating the Product Vision and the Product Goal to make sure that everyone understands the overall objective and is aligned around the work that is to be performed.

- Prioritizing and ordering the Product Backlog so that the work performed by the Scrum Team delivers the highest value to the customers and to the business.

- Refining and clearly articulating the Product Backlog Items so that the Developers on the team know not only what to do, but also why their work is important.

- Tracking progress toward a release of the product and decide when to release it.

The **Product Manager** is typically considered a broader role. The Product Manager has three main areas of responsibility:

- Understanding the market and the customers: This includes competitor analysis and strategy, customer discovery, financial projections of the product (sales, ROI, etc.), strategic fit within the organization, and understanding of the problem that customers need to solve.

- Driving execution of the product: This includes articulating a Product Vision, creating a Roadmap, defining a Release Plan, prioritizing a high-level backlog of Epics and Features, and working with the development teams to build the product and to track the progress.

- Measuring the outcomes: This includes defining metrics that can measure the value that is delivered (to the customer, to the business, or to the team), setting up key benchmarks to evaluate the performance of the product, defining the go-to-market strategy, and evaluating the product-market fit and the performance in the market.

How these roles intersect, often depends on the scale of the organization or of the product that is being built. For example:

– For a small startup, a Product Manager may also be the Product Owner, working with the Scrum Team to build the product.

– For a complex product, there may be one Product Manager and multiple Product Owners, each focused on a functional area of the overall product.

– A Chief Product Owner or a Director of Product may have the Product Manager's responsibilities, including the financial performance and budgeting for the product.

– In SAFe (Scaled Agile Framework for the enterprise) the Product Manager is a role at the Program Level who is responsible for identifying and for refining Features in the Program Backlog, whereas the Product Owner is at the Agile Team level and is responsible for Stories in the Team Backlog.

Even when working at different levels, Product Managers and Product Owners should collaborate on discovery activities, planning, priorities, and so forth. The Product Owners should not be just order takers and execute the work given by the Product Manager; they should own their piece of the product by interacting directly with their customers, creating the vision, managing the roadmap, and deciding the priorities for the product (or feature set) that they own. This creates a healthier relationship between Product Owners and Product Managers and creates an overall better product definition.

#15

WHAT IS THE
DIFFERENCE BETWEEN
A PRODUCT OWNER
AND A PROJECT
MANAGER ?

The Product Owner and the Project Manager are very different roles. The first one exists in the context of a Scrum Team and their responsibility is to drive the development of a product. The Project Manager role, on the contrary, typically is responsible for planning, organizing, and directing the completion of specific projects while ensuring that these projects are on time, on budget, and within scope. While the two roles intersect in some aspects of their job, there are a few key differences:

A **Project Manager** manages projects. A project is work that has a specific objective and typically has a start and an end, and is carefully planned for execution. Typically, with a project, there is a clear definition of everything that needs to be done, and a plan is created upfront to execute the work. The plan aims at providing clarity about what will be delivered by a specified date in time.

A **Product Owner** manages products. A product is the result of the work done by the team and it delivers an outcome for the end users. A product is created, maintained, and supported by solving problems and by providing benefits to specific customer and business users. Its planning is not done all up-front, but rather emerges from doing the work and learning more about what customers need. As such, a product may be composed over time by completing multiple projects. A product may start, but may not have a defined end.

A Product Owner and a Project Manager differ in skills and attitudes:

– A Project Manager is skilled at identifying all of the work that needs to be done, at properly planning the work, and at tracking execution toward a specific completion point and timeline. Planning, execution, and predictability are key strengths.

– A Product Owner is skilled at understanding customer needs and problems to solve, and then defining what type of work should be accomplished to address these needs. Because the discovery may not happen all at once, the Product Owner deals with ambiguity and continually prioritizes the work to maximize the value delivered. While a product may be built with a timeline in mind, the primary goal is to solve problems and to deliver value to the customers.

#16

I DO NOT HAVE TECHNICAL EXPERTISE. CAN I BE A PRODUCT OWNER ?

A Product Owner operates at the intersection of the HBT triangle – Human, Business, Technology. These areas allow the Product Owner to develop an understanding of desirability (Human = customer needs), viability (Business = business opportunity), and feasibility (Technology = building the solution). A good Product Owner has experience and knowledge in each of these areas.

When we say technology experience, we do not expect a Product Owner to be able to write code or to set up a distributed cloud architecture. The Developers can do this; after all, it is their expertise. When we say technology, we mean that

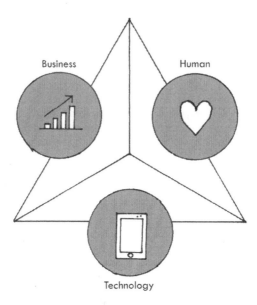

Business

Human

Technology

the Product Owner understands the domain of the product, without the need to be an expert at actually building it.

For example, if you are a Product Owner building a self-driving car, it is expected that you understand the domain not only of the car market, but more specifically of the self-driving space.

Separately, if a Product Owner is building a new web application, we would expect them to know the difference between an API and an IPA (hint: one allows writing applications; the other is a beer that you drink at happy hours).

Some of the best Product Owners we have worked with, did not have a technical background, but they had domain experience in the industry coupled with an innate curiosity to learn new things and to understand how things work, and this allowed them to connect and to quickly relate to the work that the Developers were doing.

If you are a Product Owner with limited technical background, do not worry. Your job is to focus on the market, on the customer needs, and on valuable product decisions for your business. You can always rely on the rest of the team for technical expertise, suggestions, and analyses of dependencies.

#17

CAN I INVITE MY STAKEHOLDERS TO THE BACKLOG REFINEMENT SESSION ?

The purpose of refinements is to get Product Backlog Items ready to be worked on by the Scrum Team in an upcoming Sprint. Refinement is a continuous activity for the Product Owner who talks with Stakeholders, updates the backlog, prioritizes the work items, splits the big items into smaller ones, and makes sure that each work item is properly understood by everyone involved in the product development effort. The Product Owner may do this alone or in collaboration with others. Typically, the Product Owner may work with one or more Developers to refine some of the items in the backlog, typically those that are more technical in nature or that may be too complex and require splitting into multiple smaller chunks of work. The Scrum Team decides how to do this to the best of their abilities, and typically it may take the form of a weekly meeting with some or all of the Developers to review the Product Backlog Items, to estimate the work, and to create context for the upcoming Sprints.

Since the Product Owner represents both the business and the customers to the Scrum Team, Stakeholders are not necessary. The Product Owner can provide their point of view and offer insights on expectations (or at least should be empowered to do so). If Stakeholders can offer a perspective that helps the Scrum Team, they can be invited. More than Stakeholders, I prefer to invite what I define as partners or as Subject Matter Experts. These could be members of other teams, or departments on which my team depends to get the work done. My goal is to give them an advance read of what is coming up in our backlog so that in turn they can start planning their work and prepare to support us.

REAL STORY

When I was at Capital One, the Marketing team had one month lead time to procure new photos for our apps. Whenever we started the work on a item that required a photo, we reached out to Marketing for a new photo and they said: "Sure, we can get you the new file; we just need one month to procure it."

Since our Sprints were two weeks long, we would fail the Sprint (no file was available) and we would have to wait for two more Sprints before being able to complete the work.

This changed when I started inviting Marketing to our bi-weekly refinement meetings. I offered everyone a look at what was coming up in our backlog for the next 2-3 Sprints, so that they could put in motion any process they needed to have in place to support us, like, for example, sourcing a new photo.

Because of this early alignment on future work, when we were ready to begin the work in a Sprint for a work item that needed a new photo, we knew that Marketing already had the photo available.

#18

I AM A TECHNICAL PRODUCT OWNER. IS IT OK TO BE INVOLVED IN DISCUSSING THE "HOW" ?

In a Scrum Team, the Developers are responsible for creating the solution and for identifying all of the details of how they are going to build it. By empowering the Developers to own the "how," you create the space that allows them to be successful, to take responsibility for the work they do, and to identify different, innovative solutions.

This does not mean that you delegate to the Developers every single technical decision. In fact, the key is to create collaboration within the Scrum Team. A technical Product Owner can be a valuable asset to a Scrum Team and yet they should be mindful of creating a space of collaboration with the

Developers rather than providing top-down directives about technical solutions.

When the Product Owner has a technical background or the expertise to participate in technical discussions, they can offer ideas on possible solutions, and insights about technical expectations for the product. Sometimes, a product needs to be built in a very specific way to integrate with other pieces of a larger product or with existing solutions that the customer is already using. The Product Owner makes sure that these expectations are clearly understood by the team.

Think about a team that is building a set of APIs (Application Programming Interface) to provide access to a database while also shielding the system from malicious attacks. A particular encryption mechanism for the data, or a 2-way authentication method, may be a technical requirement that the Product Owner ensures gets incorporated into the discussion. The Product Owner may provide guidance and make sure that the team is aware of the requirements, and then can leave the team alone to define the best solution and how to build it.

#19

WHAT IS THE DIFFERENCE BETWEEN PRODUCT VISION, PRODUCT GOAL, AND STRATEGY?

The **Product Vision** paints the picture of how your product will impact the world for the better if you succeed. It is the long-term objective you want to achieve with your product, the sort of North Star that guides your product development activities. It ultimately answers the following questions:

- Where are you going and what story are you telling about the future?

- Who are the people whom you will serve and who do you want your customers to become?

- What problems are you going to solve?

- What value will you deliver?

- What types of services will you offer?

- How is it better than what exists today?

The **Product Goal** is a step toward achieving the Product Vision. For large or complex products, the Product Vision may not be achieved all at once. You may achieve an initial Product Goal, and then set off to the next one, and so on, until the overarching Vision is completed. The Product Goal helps to align, to prioritize, and to determine the Product Backlog Items in your backlog: they should all consistently align to the Product Goal that you want to achieve. Once that goal is completed, your backlog will contain a new set of PBIs (Product Backlog Items), all aligned to a new Product Goal.

The **Product Strategy** defines the steps used to bring a Product Vision to life, to build the product, and to achieve the outcomes that your customers desire. The Product Strategy answers the question: "How are you going to realize your Vision?" Depending on the environment in which you operate, it keeps in consideration what you need to execute the work and to bring the Product Vision to reality – for example, key milestones you want to achieve, different versions of the product to create, resources, target segments, competitors, market forces, channels and distribution, and so forth.

#20

DO I NEED TO GET ALL OF THE UI SPECIFIED BEFORE A SPRINT, OR CAN THE DEVELOPERS DESIGN THE UI AS PART OF THE WORK THEY ARE DOING IN THE SPRINT?

The first thing to consider in answering this question is that the Scrum Team is cross-functional: its members have all of the skills and expertise needed to bring a product idea to life. Depending on the type of work you do, the team may include software developers, testers, designers, attorneys, marketing people, business analysts, and engineers.

If the design of a UI is part of the work that the Scrum Team needs to do to build a product (e.g., a new website or a new app), then a designer should be part of the Scrum Team, and the UI design should be part of the work for the Sprint. Therefore, it should be included in the work selected in the Sprint Backlog.

In practice, I often see the UI work treated in two possible ways:

- A PBI is selected for the Sprint and it requires analysis, design, development, and testing. All of the work is taken on by members of the Scrum Team who work collaboratively on diverse aspects of the PBI. If work is needed on the UI, it is done during the Sprint while other Developers work on other aspects. All of the work on the PBI is completed by the end of the Sprint.

- UI design is treated as a separate PBI on its own. This is often the case when UI work is more complex and may require prototype testing or user validation, pushing the ability of the designers on the team to complete everything within the Sprint. Often, designers perform this work in a Sprint before the one that Developers use to complete the work.

The first scenario, where all work on a PBI is completed within a Sprint, is what the Scrum Team should aim for, creating a true sense of collaboration within the team and for delivering workable PBIs at the end of the Sprint in small increments.

The second scenario, while at times unavoidable, risks creating the understanding that designers work separately from the rest of the Scrum Team and cause the design work to be done in phases before other work is taken on by the team.

#21

IS THE PRODUCT OWNER A MANDATORY ATTENDEE FOR THE DAILY SCRUM ?

The purpose of the Daily Scrum is to inspect progress toward completing the work in the Sprint Backlog to achieve the Sprint Goal and to update the plan on a daily basis. Because the Developers are the ones doing the work, they are the ones who should participate in the Daily Scrum. At the Daily Scrum, the Developers sync up with each other on what to do to move forward with the work, and to plan what to do for the next 24 hours.

– The Product Owner is optional: since the Product Owner is not doing the work during the Sprint, they do not need to be there. However, it is a good practice for the Product Owner to attend as an observer. This provides them with the opportunity to be aware of the progress the Developers are making during the Sprint and possibly any obstacles they are facing in achieving the Sprint Goal.

– Having the Product Owner attend the Daily Scrum may also help the Developers get clarification on the work items and request support for impediments. Quick decisions can be made without having to schedule a separate meeting.

– However, the presence of the Product Owner at the Daily Scrum should not be interpreted as the opportunity to provide an update to the Product Owner or to request details on the work to be done. Since the purpose of the Daily Scrum is for the Developers to inspect their progress toward the Sprint Goal and to make a plan on how to complete the work they have selected for the Sprint, it is for the Developers, and not for the Product Owner. So, if any detailed conversation needs to happen with the Product Owner, I recommend that this conversation takes place separately from the Daily Scrum. After all, the Product Owner is a member of the Scrum Team and should be readily available during the day to support the Developers in doing their work. The Daily Scrum is not that time.

– Even if the Product Owner is unavailable for every Daily Scrum meeting, just having them sporadically attend the meeting reduces the need for separate status meetings and provides context to the Product Owner on where the Developers are with their work. There are no surprises during the Sprint as the Product Owner is in the loop on how the Sprint is progressing.

#22

WHEN IS THE RIGHT TIME FOR THE PRODUCT OWNER TO INTERACT WITH THE TEAM ?

We often see Product Owners who interact with the rest of the team only at the Scrum events. The Product Owner participates at Sprint Planning, working together with the Developers at creating the Sprint Goal and the Sprint Backlog. And they may attend the Daily Scrum, listening in to what the team is doing and to any impediments they may face. Then, the Product Owner disappears in their cubicle and eagerly awaits the Sprint Review to see what the team has achieved during the Sprint and to give their sign of approval. And they may sit in the Retrospective half-heartedly providing their opinion on what the team could improve. The Sprint is over, and the next one repeats the same pattern: The Product Owner uses the Scrum events to interact with the Developers and to give "marching orders," while the rest of the time they are absent from the Scrum Team.

We have seen this pattern in many Scrum Teams we have worked with, especially in situations where the Product Owner is from one company, and the Developers are hired contractors from another company. It is a limited view of the role of the Product Owner and of its relationship with the rest of the Scrum Team.

Let us begin by saying that the Product Owner is a member of the Scrum Team, and not an external figure that "interacts" with the team. As a member of the team, they should work side by side with everyone else on the team throughout the Sprint. Clearly, they have different responsibilities than the Developers, but this does not mean that the Product Owner should wear the invisibility cloak during the Sprint and wait for the "demo" to see the product increment. Instead, they should collaborate with the Developers every day, providing context on the objectives of the work, on the customer needs, and on the expected outcomes of the work. They should review the work completed as it gets done, asking the Developers to revisit or to update it right away if anything seems not perfect – and not wait until the Sprint Review to do so. In essence, the Product Owner should work side by side with the rest of the Scrum Team, and not in a separate "bubble" waiting for the next Scrum event.

Refinement is another opportunity to collaborate with the Developers, giving the team an opportunity to inspect the Product Backlog, to get an early read of the work that is prioritized for upcoming Sprints, and to work with them to break down larger items of work into smaller ones.

And finally, we invite Product Owners to create opportunities to connect the Developers to the Stakeholders and to the customers. By having direct visibility and understanding of the customer needs and the market context in which the team is operating, the Developers can contribute ideas and support the Product Owner in product decisions – rather than having the Product Owner make all of the decisions on their own. One way to do this is to invite the Developers - maybe one at a time on a rotational basis – to join the Product Owner in customer discovery activities, such as interviews or usability testing.

REAL STORY

Years ago, I was a Product Owner and I sat on the 3rd floor where all of the product and businesspeople were situated. The rest of my development team sat on the 8th floor of the same building.

A couple of times a day I took the elevator and went up to interact with the Developers of my team. However, there were times when I was busy doing my own work, or in conversations with other business stakeholders, and maybe a whole day or two passed before I showed up upstairs.

During one Retrospective, it emerged that my limited availability had an adverse effect on the rest of the team: sometimes they had a question for me or needed clarification on some details of the work, and they waited patiently for me to show up. Or they wrote me an email, but if I was busy, I would not answer it right away. They waited for me, slowing down their work and wasting time.

We discussed different ideas on how to address these problems, and it became clear that the best solution would be for me to move up to the 8th floor. After asking HR, I was told that no desk was available on that floor. So, I took my desk from the 3rd floor, put it in the elevator, and moved upstairs next to my Scrum Team.

This improved the communication channel as I was readily available to answer any questions or to provide context around any work item, avoiding unnecessary delays in communication. On the other hand, it put a bit of strain on my relationship with the rest of the product and businesspeople , and I resorted to taking the elevator down to the 3rd floor whenever possible.

#23

MY TEAM IS SLACKING. HOW DO I KNOW IF THEY ARE PUTTING IN THEIR BEST EFFORT AND IS THERE A WAY TO MEASURE THE PERFORMANCE OF THE SCRUM TEAM?

There are plenty of data points that can be used to measure the performance of a team. In general, we are advocates for quality versus quantity, and for measuring productivity based on outcomes produced rather than hours worked.

In this context, you can look at different metrics to evaluate productivity for your team, such as:

– **Quality of the work done by the team during the Sprint.** Does the work satisfy the Definition of Done (DoD) for the team? Is there any rework that needs to happen, and that may slow down the team in future Sprints? In addition to measuring adherence to the DoD, you can look at metrics like the number of defects introduced, the number of tests failed, and integration issues.

– **Involvement of the team during the various Scrum meetings.** Is everyone fully participating? Is every team member empowered and heard during the meetings?

– **The team's ability to deliver valuable work consistently during each Sprint.** Is the team delivering the outcomes that customers expect? You can use the Sprint Review effectively to validate the work done with stakeholders and collect their feedback. And then use the Retro to discuss within the Scrum Team, what to change or to improve to satisfy the expectations of stakeholders in future Sprints.

– **Velocity measures improve.** The team increases velocity over time as the team improves their performance and gets better at doing the work.

In addition, we have often seen that when teams overcommit, struggle with multitasking, or are not given clear priorities, they tend to struggle to get work done, feel overstressed, and in general have low productivity. When this is the case, rather than adding pressure to the team, the best solution is to help the team implement some of the successful Scrum patterns. Here are a few examples of what to look for and what you can implement to help your team improve productivity:

– **The Sprint Goal success:** are you delivering work aligned with the Sprint Goal and do you do it consistently during each Sprint? Does the team complete 100% of their Sprint Backlog in most of the Sprints? Or is the team taking on too much work during each Sprint? A common pattern for productive teams is the *Interrupt Pattern*[1]. This requires having a buffer in capacity during each Sprint. For example, you may decide to leave 15 points unplanned during every Sprint (or whatever number of points creates enough buffer for your team). If the Developers complete all of the work in the Sprint Backlog and they have spare time before the Sprint ends, they can use the buffer to do more work. Just ask the Product Owner what is next in the backlog. Having a buffer creates slack in the team's commitment, allowing them to deal with unexpected work requests that otherwise would disrupt the work of the Sprint.

– **Team's morale.** The team's Happiness Metric can provide insights into how the team is feeling. Often, an underperforming team suffers from stress, from low morale, and from conflicting priorities. Measure the Happiness Metric and track it over time. Often, a drop in this metric can be a leading indicator of a drop of performance, and if you catch it early, you may help the team get back on track.

– **Team's total motivation.** In "Primed to Perform"[2] the authors describe 3 dimensions that contribute to the team's Total Motivation score (ToMo) in a positive way, and they are: Play, Purpose, and Potential. Is your team aligned to these dimensions?

– **Frequency of team members being replaced on the team.** *Stable Teams* is a common pattern for highly productive teams (low attrition is better). Using Tuckman's stages of team development (Forming, Storming, Norming, Performing), the goal of a productive team is to get to the Performing stage. But every time a new team member leaves the team or a new one is added, the team is brought back to Forming. Rather than forming a new team for each new project, consider creating Stable Teams that work together for a long period of time, and bring different projects to the team.

REFERENCES

1. Teams that Finish Early Accelerate Faster: A Pattern Language for High Performing Scrum Teams https://www.scruminc.com/wp-content/uploads/2014/05/teamsthatfinishearlyacceleratefaster.pdf
2. "Primed to Perform" by Lindsay McGregor and Neel Doshi

#24

HOW DO I KEEP MY
STAKEHOLDERS
UPDATED ON
PROGRESS TOWARD
THE RELEASE WHEN
THINGS ARE
CONSTANTLY
CHANGING?

One of the Agile Values is: "*Responding to change over following a plan.*"[1] While plans and having a plan are a good thing, we should set the expectation with everyone involved in the product development effort, including Stakeholders, that the plans will change.

The key is to create transparency on both the plan and on the progress you are making. For example, share a Release Plan and track progress toward the release using a Release Burn-Up chart. The Burn-up should be updated at least once per Sprint by the Product Owner using the actual velocity of the team in that Sprint and the work completed. If any deviation from the target is identified, the Product Owner should immediately create transparency with the Stakeholders. This could happen at a minimum at Sprint Review as the progress toward the release is a useful topic of conversation at that event.

When progress toward the release deviates from the initial expectations, the Product Owner can discuss with the Stakeholders what to do, and typically there are three levers that can be pulled:

Adjust timeline. If the release plan shows that you are running late, discuss extending the timeline. Use the current velocity of the team to project out how long it will take to complete all of the work, and establish a new (possible) release date. The conversation should be something like, "Stakeholders, given our current progress and projected velocity, we will not be able to complete all of the work we had planned by the deadline. In fact, we will need an extra X weeks to complete the release. Are you OK with this extended deadline?"

Adjust scope. When the timeline is fixed and the Burn-up chart shows that you will not be able to complete all of the work in time, consider adjusting the scope of the work. Create transparency about progress and expected completion rate with the Stakeholders, and then invite them to consider reducing the scope. The conversation should be something like, "Stakeholders, given our current progress and projected velocity, we will not be able to complete all of the work we had planned by the deadline. What can we prioritize and what can we remove from this release, so that we can complete it by the deadline?" The work that gets deprioritized will be completed in a future release, giving the opportunity to the team to focus on what is essential for this release.

Adjust capacity. When the timeline is fixed and the scope is also fixed (your Stakeholders want it all, and want it on time) then the only remaining lever is capacity. If you were able to increase capacity, then you may be able to finish all of the work by the deadline.

Working overtime is not a solution. It may work short-term, or give the false impression of increased productivity. The reality is that it is not a sustainable pace.

Compromising on quality also is not a good solution. You can take a shortcut, compromise technical quality, and deliver faster. Sometimes, this may be a reasonable path, especially when the value of delivering early is higher than the cost of fixing the problems later. The problem is the technical debt. When you accumulate technical debt, finishing on time becomes a mirage. You move toward your goal, but you are not really reaching the goal: the technical debt prevents you from considering the work really complete because the shortcuts you took to get there will have to be addressed in the future. And all of the rework is going to slow you down.

The solution should be increased capacity. How to do that, you may ask. More people. Maybe another team. With higher overall capacity, you can do more work faster and finish earlier. Of course, adding new people is not an immediate solution, nor is adding a team. It takes time to onboard people and to bring them up to speed. So, the sooner you create transparency around your needs and bring in more people, the faster you will be at ramping up capacity.

REFERENCES

1. Manifesto for Agile Software Development—https://agilemanifesto.org/

#25

WHEN SHOULD WE INVOLVE THE SUBJECT MATTER EXPERTS (SME) DURING THE SPRINT?

A great opportunity to involve the Subject Matter Experts (SMEs) is your backlog refinement session. How often you do it depends on decisions made by your team and can be once per Sprint or more frequently. The point is that when you do a refinement meeting with the Scrum Team, to look at the upcoming backlog and to make sure everyone understands the work to be done, that is a great opportunity to invite the SMEs and to align with them.

The SMEs can provide additional context or details on the work that needs to be done, strengthening the understanding and helping the Developers be better prepared. The SMEs can also contribute to the understanding of the Acceptance Criteria or the DoD.

At times, the SMEs may be a dependency for the work you do during the Sprint – for example, the SMEs may provide security review of the work you complete. The refinement sessions are very useful since they ascertain that the SMEs know what you are going to work on in a future Sprint, and can properly plan how to support you during that Sprint.

If useful, you can also invite them to Sprint Planning meetings. This creates transparency among everyone involved in the work and ensures that work schedules and expectations are aligned.

CASE STUDY

A few years ago, I was working as a Product Owner for a top 10 bank in the United States. My team and I were building a series of software applications that our bankers used to interact with customers and to explain different financial products. In the United States there is a regulation called the Americans with Disabilities Act (ADA) that requires applications to be usable by customers who may have a disability, like limited vision or color blindness. There are criteria to measure if the application is compliant or not, and the bank employed a team of ADA experts whose job was to support the software teams in making the right design choices.

My team and I were not experts in ADA, so we invited the ADA experts to guide us. We found that the best opportunity to involve the experts was during our weekly refinement session.

During these refinement sessions, we reviewed the Product Backlog Items that we expected to work on in the next 2-3 Sprints, provided clarification about our intent, and asked the experts for any advice on what to cover and how to properly create the functionality we expected to deliver. These refinement sessions were highly productive, and allowed everybody to get an early read of the upcoming work so that we could all be aligned and knew what to expect.

In our case, we also needed to pass a formal "ADA review" for every work item that we completed during the Sprint. This required sending the end result of our work to the ADA experts and giving them a couple of days to review it. Because we had done refinement together, the ADA experts knew what we were working on, and this sped up their review process when they received the work we completed.

#26

CAN SCRUM BE USED OUTSIDE OF SOFTWARE DEVELOPMENT?

Scrum is a framework that can be, and is being used, outside of software development all the time. It provides the team with a structure within which the team has all of the flexibility to develop complex products.

It is true that the origins of Scrum are in software development. In fact, Jeff Sutherland and Ken Schwaber (the creators of Scrum, 1994-95) faced a challenge while building a new software product for the company they were working on. They started experimenting with a few different methods, and ultimately created Scrum. Since then, Scrum has become the most widely adopted agile framework in the world.

But, successful use of Scrum is not limited to software teams. For example, legal, marketing, hardware teams around the world have found the simplicity and effectiveness of Scrum useful to drive productivity, to create transparency within the team, and to validate the work they are doing.

EXAMPLE

We use Scrum to manage the work of our company, and we do 1-week Sprints. My partner and I recognized that we were slow at making progress in a variety of projects that we wanted to complete, like writing a book, setting up the website for our company, and preparing a set of videos. We decided to start managing our company using Scrum, and we now do 1-week Sprints. On Mondays, we do Sprint Planning, selecting work items from the Product Backlog and agreeing on what we want to accomplish for the week. Then, everybody gets to work, and we keep each other updated throughout the Sprint on progress and on any obstacles we are facing. On Fridays, we do a Sprint Review to discuss what we accomplished, and decide what can be done next. And then we do a quick Retrospective to discover any opportunities for improvement.

Since we started organizing our work this way, we have sped up the work, completed several of the projects, and most importantly, we feel more like a team rather than two individuals rowing in all directions without a specific goal in mind.

#27

SHOULD THE PRODUCT OWNER STAY FOR THE ENTIRE SPRINT PLANNING?

While the Product Owner is needed in the first part of Sprint Planning when the Scrum Team decides what to do in the Sprint and aligns on the Sprint Goal, the Product Owner does not have an active role in the second part of the event. Here, the Developers prepare a plan for the execution of the work they selected for the Sprint. They identify dependencies, order of the work, details of the execution, eventual additional assets needed, and break down the work into manageable activities.

The Product Owner's presence during the second part of Sprint Planning may be useful in order to clarify details or to answer the Developers' question on any work item selected for the Sprint and the expected outcome of the work. So, while not strictly needed, it is useful for the Product Owner to attend the entire event to ensure a productive completion of Sprint Planning.

#28

WHAT IS THE
DIFFERENCE BETWEEN
A GANTT CHART AND
A ROADMAP?

For people familiar with project management, the Gantt Chart is a tool used to visualize the activities that take place in the project and in their timeline. Each activity, or task, is represented with a horizontal bar, showing when the activity is scheduled to start and to end. It is named after its inventor, Henry Gantt, who designed this chart around the years 1910–15. The Gantt Chart is often used to show the dependencies and relationships between activities. It is typically detailed enough to identify the tasks that need to be completed, and often contains dates for the start and the end of each activity. It can also represent the current schedule status by marking in different colors, activities that may be running late or are impeded. The Gantt Chart is a representation of what gets done and how.

While the Gantt Chart is used to visualize activities and their relationships, a Product Roadmap serves a different purpose. Both tools display information related to completing a long-term project, such as developing a product. They also set milestones for various aspects of the project over time. Where they differ, is in the strategic alignment.

The goal of the Product Roadmap is to provide a strategic map on how to execute the Product Vision. We can think of the roadmap as that link that connects the Product Vision to the strategy, showing concrete steps to execute the work and to achieve the goal. In practice, a Product Roadmap identifies a few broad time periods (e.g., the next 6 months, or the next 4 quarters in a year, or "Now, Next, Later" periods) and maps out what our Stakeholders are going to get in each period, in terms of features and outcomes. In fact, good roadmaps not only show the list of features that the team will deliver in each period, but also show the objectives the team aims to achieve with these features. In essence, the Product Roadmap focuses on the what and on the why.

In product management, planning out a series of activities with a level of granularity and predefined timelines as specified in a Gantt Chart, can be both a daunting undertaking, and a useless effort. In a world where markets change rapidly, customer needs may not be fully understood, and products are developed through rapid experimentation, the certainty conveyed by a Gantt Chart is often too distant from reality to make the tool useful.

Instead, Product Roadmaps define a higher level of details, give indicative timelines, and paint a picture in broad strokes – rather than precise details. The fourth Agile value states that we value more "Responding to change over following the plan" and Product Roadmaps support this value. They represent a plan – and a plan is useful and important to have to share where we are heading and how – and at the same time, they allow for changes and updates as the team learns more and adapts the plan.

In fact, it is also important for Stakeholders to consider the Product Roadmap – and any plan for that matter – as something that is not carved in stone, but rather can be adapted and changed over time. A plan is the team's best attempt at predicting the future based on the information we have today. But we know that we – as humans – are not very good at predicting the future (if we were, everyone would have Bitcoins, President Trump would not have surprised the world with his election victory in 2016 against Hillary Clinton, and Covid would not have brought havoc around the world). If we are not good at predicting the future, and roadmaps represent the future, then we should expect that things are going to be different from what we expected, and we need to be able to update the roadmap.

#29

WHO SHOULD APPLY PRESSURE TO THE TEAM TO GET THEM TO TAKE ON MORE WORK ?

When pressure exceeds a peak point, it has the opposite effect and the team's performance begins to decline as a result. Applying pressure does not work and does not yield results the way we like to think. Burnt out teams have the highest attrition rate, low team morale, and no motivation to innovate or to contribute to the team.

Self-organized teams perform far better because as humans we are motivated by autonomy. When the team is self-managed, they take ownership of the Goal; they feel like contributing and putting in their best effort. In fact, we should create an environment that enables the team to perform at their best by doing the following:

– Help them stay focused on the prioritized items, by properly prioritizing the backlog and establishing a capacity buffer every Sprint.

– Provide additional help if the Developers are overwhelmed (provide efficient tools and bring in Subject Matter Experts, etc.)

– If there is a particular area that the team is struggling with, then maybe provide training, workshops and so forth. Help address those impediments.

– Provide frequent breaks to avoid burnout – take a day off or go for a walk or step away from the desk at regular intervals, listen to an amusing podcast while enjoying a cup of coffee, and so forth.

– Make the team members aware of wellness programs that your office may offer.

– Find ways to lighten the mood of the team – watching amusing videos together, cooking the same dish and exchanging recipes, scheduling some icebreaker activities, and trying different flavored popcorn together while seeing some team members cringe at certain strong flavors.

– During Retrospectives, address issues openly and create an environment of psychological safe space which encourages people to have honest conversations with each other.

30

WHAT IS THE DIFFERENCE BETWEEN SCRUM AND AGILE ?

Synonyms of agile: nimble, quick-moving, and adaptive. We want our leaders and team members to become agile. They should be able to respond to changes.

The relationship between Agile and Scrum is intertwined in that one influences the other and vice versa.

– **Scrum**: launched in 1995 by Jeff Sutherland and Ken Schwaber, based on principles derived from Lean manufacturing and ideas presented in "The New Product Development Game" by Hirotaka Takeuchi and Ikujiro Nonaka[1].

– **Agile Manifesto**: set of 4 Values and 12 Principles formalized in 2001, by 18 innovators in the software development space. The experience developed using Scrum in the previous years had a strong influence on the Agile Manifesto[2], as did ideas from Extreme Programming and Lean. When we talk about Agile we refer to the set of values and principles presented in the Agile Manifesto. Various frameworks exist that apply the Agile values and principles and bring them to reality, and one of them is Scrum.

Also, see the interview with Jeff Sutherland at the beginning of this book for more insights on the origins of Scrum.

REFERENCES

1. "The New Product Development Game" by Hirotaka Takeuchi and Ikujiro Nonaka - https://hbr.org/1986/01/the-new-new-product-development-game
2. Manifesto for Agile Software Development—https://agilemanifesto.org/

#31

SHOULD WE ASSIGN WORK TO THE MOST ABLE DEVELOPER FOR THAT SPECIFIC WORK TYPE, TO INCREASE EFFICIENCY?

There are a few ways to think about this:

– **The phantom of efficiency:** One way to look at this is the trade-off between short-term gain versus long-term team development. By giving the work to the most able Developer, you get it done, probably quicker and more efficiently. And sometimes this is needed. However, what are you losing? I would say that by treating your top performers as your stars, you risk compromising long-term team development. The other

Developers are given easier or simpler work, and by avoiding the challenge, they do not get to learn as much. You also risk overloading your top performers with too much work or responsibilities, causing attrition and ultimately slowing down the overall performance of the team. The goal should be skill development so that over time, the entire team rises and becomes a team of stars. One way to do this is to use Pair Programming (two people working together on the same task). Another way is to alternate who does what during each Sprint so that everybody gets a chance to work on all of the activities.

– **The team should be cross-functional and self-organizing:** The Developers should decide who does what and divide the work among themselves as they see fit. They should strive for achieving the Sprint Goal, satisfying the quality standards of the DoD, and supporting skill development within the team. The goal is not efficiency. It is the quality of the product and the outcomes it delivers.

– **Look at the efficiency of the team as a whole, not of the individual:** This concept comes from System Thinking, the idea that we should look at optimizing the whole system, rather than individual components. If you think about it, it makes sense: when you optimize one individual component in a system, this does nothing to change the performance of other components which may still be bottlenecks. You improve one piece of the system, but the overall performance has not changed.

The Scrum Team can be thought of as a system. To improve the performance of the team, sometimes you need to de-optimize the individual performance. For example, if Mike has a problem and reaches out to Holly for help, but Holly is fully utilized, she will not be able to help Mike, and he will fall behind in his work. As a result, the performance of the whole team will suffer. Instead, if all of the members of the team have slack in their schedule, then they can help each other when needed, thereby improving the performance of the team. So, when looking at improving the performance of the team, find ways to help every member to elevate their performance, to grow as professionals, and to develop their skill set. It is not about pushing people to do more work; it is about helping everyone grow. The team as a whole will then grow.

#32

OUR DAILY SCRUM
RUNS FOR AN HOUR.
HOW DO I BRING IT
DOWN TO 15
MINUTES **?**

The first thing you should do is to make sure that everyone understands the purpose of the Daily Scrum. You will be surprised by the number of team members who may not know the purpose of this meeting. Some think it is about providing status updates. Some think it is for the Scrum Master to know how the team is doing. Others think it is all about answering three questions. In reality, none of these are true.

As the Scrum Master, you can help the team understand that this is an inspection and planning meeting and not a status or solutioning meeting.

The purpose of the Daily Scrum is for the Developers to inspect the progress of their work and to make a plan for what to do today to advance toward the Sprint Goal. It is not about the past (status); it is about the future (plan). Also, it is not about detailed discussions on the solution or on the impediments. There is not enough time for this. But there is enough time for deciding what to do today, as a team, in order to advance the work toward the Sprint Goal.

You should teach the Developers the Daily Scrum and make sure that everyone understands the purpose. Share the page from the Scrum Guide with the team members and have a conversation about the Daily Scrum. In addition to teaching, I would also suggest conducting 1-to-1 coaching sessions and group coaching.

Also, try using different techniques to facilitate the conversation: 3 Questions and Popcorn Technique, or PBI-by-PBI Review help make the meeting shorter by providing a structure to be followed.

What if we need to discuss details of the implementation or how to address requirements in our solution?

Since the Daily Scrum is timeboxed at 15 minutes, there is not enough time to discuss details or solutions. Our suggestion is to focus the Daily Scrum on its purpose, by updating the plan for the work to do today. Then, if needed, a few team members can stay back after the Daily Scrum and help resolve the impediments or discuss details of the implementation. This can be a "Meet After" event.

#33

WE HAVE LOTS OF IDEAS DURING THE RETROSPECTIVE, BUT WE CANNOT DECIDE WHICH ONE TO FOCUS ON. HOW TO DECIDE NEXT STEPS?

First of all, I think it is a very good sign that you have a team that feels like sharing new ideas. It is a sign of a positive and safe environment!

It is important to end the Retrospective with at least one action item – something to work on to improve the team and to support Kaizen (a Japanese term meaning change for the better or continuous improvement). However, having too many action items generates confusion and a lack of focus, often resulting in no improvement whatsoever. So, when you have many ideas, it is a good thing to prioritize them and to pick one or two to act upon. Do this together with the team, so that everyone has a voice in the decision-making process.

The following are a few popular techniques that can help your team come to a consensus on what to do next. These are fun, simple, and effective:

Dot Voting – Participants vote on the available options using a limited number of stickers or marks with pens – dot stickers being the most common. The idea with the most dot votes is the winner.

Thumbs Up/Down or Sideways – "Thumbs Up" implies agreement. "Thumbs Down" implies disagreement. "Sideways" says "do not know/not decided." Review one item at a time and ask the team for their votes. Based on the number of thumbs up/down, one could sense peoples' decisions and you can make the final call.

Fist to Five – The team shows their support for the various options presented during the Retro by a show of different number of fingers.

- Closed Fist – No way; I have no confidence in this at all.

- 1 Finger – Major concerns.

- 2 Fingers – Minor concerns.

- 3 Fingers – Some issues, but nothing that cannot be resolved later.

- 4 Fingers – I support this.

- 5 Fingers – I love this! You have my full support.

Another important tip for the Retrospective is to change the format or structure often. Asking, "What worked/what did not work" at every Retrospective can quickly become repetitive or feel stagnant. How many new insights can you come up with by answering the same questions?

The suggestion is to change the format – potentially you can do this at each Retrospective. For example, do a Plus Delta exercise once, then at the next Sprint use the Speedboat exercise, and then use the Genie of the Lamp. These are just examples, and you may create your own list of favorite exercises. The invitation is to spend some time experimenting with different exercises and formats, and to find your favorite ways to run the Retrospective.

For ideas, we recommend reading "Project Retrospectives"[1] and "Agile Retrospectives: Making Good Teams Great"[2]. Also, great resources for ideas on Retrospective design are various websites, including Tasty Cupcakes[3] and Retromat[4].

Finally, here are a few tips to make your Retrospectives more effective:

- The Scrum Master is not the only one to facilitate. In fact, you can have team members alternate in facilitating it. Or, you can ask a Scrum Master on another team, to facilitate it for you, so that everyone on your team can participate.

- Spend at least as much time planning the Retrospective as you spend doing it. Choosing the exercise, setting up context, choosing what to focus the Retrospective on, and deciding who is going to facilitate it all, require preparation. Be sure to allocate a good amount of time to prepare before you run the Retrospective.

- Use the Retrospective not only to generate insights, but also to discuss possible solutions to most vexing problems as an opportunity for improvement. Identify one or more action items and place it in the Product Backlog, or even better, schedule it for the next Sprint.

- And, as just said, frequently change the exercise or the framework to run the Retrospective.

REFERENCES

1. "Project Retrospectives" by Norman Kerth
2. "Agile Retrospectives: Making Good Teams Great" by Esther Derby and Diana Larsen
3. Tasty Cupcakes http://tastycupcakes.org/tag/retrospective/
4. Retromat https://retromat.org/

Image by yummybuum @ Freepik

#34

SHOULD WE DO THE REFINEMENT AND SPRINT PLANNING TOGETHER ?

Refinement is not a required meeting of Scrum; however, many teams find it useful to get an early read of the future work in the backlog and to better prepare for the upcoming Sprint Planning. How and when the team does Refinement, is a choice of the Scrum Team. And it is useful to do it separately from Sprint Planning.

During **Refinement**, the team reviews, refines, and estimates the User Stories that are potential candidates for the upcoming few Sprints (the next Sprint and possibly one or two after that). Conducting Refinement sessions ensures that the team has an understanding of what they will be likely working on in an upcoming Sprint. It also provides visibility to partners about the type of work that the team will take on, and helps them prepare to support eventual dependencies (e.g., members of another team on which your team depends on can be invited at Refinement to get an idea of what work you need them to tackle before you start your Sprint). It builds transparency and confidence in the team.

Sprint Planning is a planning and confirmation meeting where the team crafts the Sprint Goal, where the Product Owner confirms the prioritized list of User Stories candidate for the Sprint, and where the Developers select how much work they can take on in the Sprint, based on their capacity. The Developers also make a plan for how to execute the work selected for the Sprint (tasks, orders, dependencies, etc.).

Refinement should not be a substitute for Sprint Planning. No decision is taken at Refinement regarding the work that will be done in the next Sprint. Instead, Refinement is used to provide visibility and to create context on the work that will likely be selected for the next few Sprints, waiting for the Sprint Planning meeting to make the final decision on what work to execute.

Combining these meetings may result in

– Forecasting items that may not have been fully reviewed due to lack of time.

– Too many activities to perform in this long meeting that may lead to meeting fatigue which is seldom productive.

– The Product Owner not having all of the details the Developers need before they can pull the work into the Sprint, so having those few days before the Sprint Planning will help the Product Owner to gather those details.

– Not enough time to discuss the strategy on how to efficiently work on those User Stories.

#35

DOES THE DEFINITION OF DONE APPLY TO THE FULL SPRINT (ALL CRITERIA FOR THE SPRINT TO BE COMPLETE); IF SO, HOW IS IT DIFFERENT FROM AN ACCEPTANCE CRITERIA ?

At the end of the Sprint the Increment must be usable. Only work that is completed is part of the Increment. Any incomplete work goes back to the Product Backlog for future evaluation. The Scrum Guide says: "Each Increment is additive to all prior Increments and thoroughly verified, ensuring that all Increments work together. In order to provide value, the Increment must be usable."

The **Definition of Done** applies to all of the work that the team is doing. It describes the conditions to validate that the Increment is usable and can be potentially released. Think about it as a list of criteria you need to check to know if the work is completed or not. The criteria include conditions on quality, integration, releasability, security – everything that the team considers important to determine the work as "done".

Acceptance Criteria are specific to one Product Backlog Item or User Story. They describe the conditions to validate the individual work item. They can also be used to test the work to determine if it's completed or not.

Definition of Done	Acceptance Criteria
It is a quality checklist that the Increment should adhere to. The DoD is additional to the Acceptance Criteria defined for a PBI. It is a common set of criteria to know when the work is done.	A confirmation from the client / user in every PBI/User Story that specifies how to test the work on the PBI. Acceptance Criteria define what "done" looks like for an individual PBI, and what needs to be demonstrated to the Product Owner in order for them to accept the work as done.
Defined by the Scrum Team from the organization's perspective.	Defined for each PBI from the customer's or user's perspective.
The DoD promotes a common set of quality criteria that all of the work done by the Scrum Team needs to adhere to. It also specifies criteria to complete before the work can be fully deployed to the user.	Acceptance Criteria promote test-driven development by making it clear how the work on the PBI should be tested. The Acceptance Criteria also help to focus the development effort on just the right amount of work to satisfy the test criteria, avoiding extra functionality.
Applicable to all the work items in the Sprint, a comprehensive quality checklist.	Unique for every PBI/User Story.
Building the Right Way.	Building the Right Thing.

#36

WHAT HAPPENS WHEN THE SCRUM MASTER IS AWAY OR ON VACATION?

The Scrum Master's role is that of a coach and as a facilitator for the Scrum Team. When they do their job effectively, the Scrum Master helps the team improve as a team and as professionals. Over time, the team improves its performance and becomes more and more a highly performing team. At that point, the team may not need as much coaching or facilitation as they needed when they just started. The team has matured and they can facilitate their own events.

With this in mind, when the Scrum Master is away or on vacation, it may become a great opportunity for the individual team members to step up and to take some of the responsibilities on their own. For example, they can facilitate the Scrum events in the absence of the Scrum Master, and practice doing it.

If you are a Scrum Master and want to coach your team on how to do this, one way to start is to ask a Developer to facilitate the Daily Scrum. It is a Developers' meeting after all, and they can self-facilitate it. Another idea is to ask a Developer to facilitate the next Retrospective. In fact, the Scrum Team members can alternate on who facilitates each event. The Scrum Master just needs to ensure that the meeting takes place and that all the participants understand its purpose.

Another idea could be that at the beginning of the project, the Scrum Team assigns backups for each other. If the Scrum Master is away or on vacation, one of the Developers volunteers to perform the role of the Scrum Master and may reduce their own current workload for that duration.

Also, you can ask a Scrum Master from another team to help your team by facilitating the various Scrum events and by removing some urgent blockers in your team's way.

#37

WHO TRACKS THE OVERALL WORK DURING THE SPRINT?

To answer this question, we should first consider why we want to track the work during the Sprint. Possible answers:

1. So that the team knows where they are in the Sprint and what is left to do in order to achieve the Sprint Goal

2. So that the Product Owner is informed of progress

3. So that the Stakeholders can receive a status update about the work

4. So that the team can win 100 points for every work item completed toward winning a Maserati car

I am of course joking about answer #4 – although I think it would be a cool idea to implement!

For answer #1, since the Developers are doing the work and they have committed to achieving the Sprint Goal, they should track their own progress during the Sprint. The Sprint Backlog and the Burn-down Chart provide visibility into the progress of the Sprint.

– The Developers are tracking their work on a daily basis. During the Daily Scrum they are updating each other on the overall progress they are making as a team toward reaching the goal of that Sprint. They use various tools to track progress (also called information radiators), for example, they can use a Burn-down Chart. This, together with the Sprint Backlog, should be visible to everyone.

– The Product Owner and the Scrum Master can review the Sprint Backlog and the Burn-down Chart to stay updated on the team's progress.

– The Scrum Master ensures that the Developers update the information radiators on a daily basis which makes tracking the overall progress easier.

For the Product Owner to be informed about the progress of the work (answer #2), they can see the Sprint Backlog and the information radiators updated by the Developers. These provide a quick glance of where the team is and whether they are on track to complete the Sprint Goal by the end of the Sprint. In addition, as we have said multiple times, the Product Owner should interact with the Developers on a regular basis (they are members of the same team after all!). And, the Product Owner can observe the Daily Scrum to get a quick read of where the team is and if they are facing any impediments.

The best way for the Stakeholders (answer #3) to get a read about the progress of the work during the Sprint, is to ask the Product Owner (after all, they should be interacting on a regular basis). Also, the Stakeholders should participate in the Sprint Review. This is the Scrum event designed for the Stakeholders so that they can interact with the Scrum Team, receive an update on the work completed, and together review the work to do next.

38

IS IT OK IF THE PRODUCT OWNER APPROVES/REJECTS THE DONE ITEMS DURING THE SPRINT REVIEW?

The short answer is no: the Product Owner needs to review and to approve the work items during the Sprint and not to wait until the end.

The purpose of the Sprint Review is to gather feedback from the key Stakeholders on the work that the Scrum Team has completed during the Sprint. In addition, the participants adapt the Product Backlog, the priorities, and the Release plan as a consequence of decisions made together during the meeting. In order for the Sprint Review to be effective, the Increment produced during the Sprint must be done, and that also means that the Product Owner has already reviewed it and approved it.

At Sprint Review, the Product Owner typically sets the stage up by performing the following activities:

– Share the Sprint Goal.

– Provide an overview of the items that were forecasted by the team for the Sprint just finished.

– Discuss what got done during the Sprint and what, if anything, was not completed.

– Talk about the Release Plan and what is coming up next in the Product Backlog.

– Discuss the overall status of the project.

So, if you want the Product Owner to be able to do the aforementioned activities effectively, it is imperative that the Product Owner has already accepted/rejected the work during the Sprint and before the Sprint Review.

Also, at the Sprint Review, typically the Developers guide the Stakeholders in a demonstration of the Increment so that the Stakeholders can experience the work done so far on the product, and provide feedback. This should not be the first time that the Product Owner sees the finished work!

Ideally, the Product Owner works side by side with the Developers during the Sprint. As the Developers complete an item of work, they check with the Product Owner for validation and for confirmation. This happens throughout the Sprint, so that when Sprint Review arrives, the whole Scrum Team can present the work completed to the Stakeholders, without surprises.

#39

DOES EVERYONE NEED TO PROVIDE AN UPDATE DURING THE DAILY SCRUM; DO WE ALL HAVE TO ANSWER THE 3 QUESTIONS?

Scrum does not mandate how you should conduct the Daily Scrum. The purpose of the Daily Scrum is for the Developers to connect with each other at least once a day, to inspect their progress toward reaching the Sprint Goal, and to update their plan for what to do today. The Daily Scrum supports the three pillars of Empiricism and the Scrum values: It helps everyone **Focus** on the Sprint Goal, communicate and provide **Transparency** on how the team is progressing cohesively during the Sprint, **Inspect** where the team is compared to the Sprint Goal they have **Committed** to, embody **Courage** by bringing up any impediments they are facing, and **Adapt** their plan for the day.

To achieve all of this, the Developers can use a variety of techniques. The 3 Questions are very popular:

1. "What did we complete yesterday toward reaching the Sprint Goal?"

2. "What are we going to complete today to advance toward reaching the Sprint Goal?

3. "Do we have any impediments?"

The 3 Questions are popular because they provide a structure to the Daily Scrum that is easy to follow, and allows everyone to participate and to have a voice. This could be useful when you have a team member who is not sharing much about their updates or conversely, when there is someone who wants to share everything they did under the sun and does not stop talking.

Although popular, the 3 Questions may not be the most effective structure to use at the Daily Scrum. For example, it is easy for the Scrum Team to follow a daily ritual where everyone answers the 3 Questions mechanically, without really focusing on the Sprint Goal and the work remaining in the Sprint to accomplish it. Everyone shares what they accomplished yesterday and what they are going to work on today, showing off how hard they are working on their individual tasks. But what is missing, is a sense of commitment together as a team in achieving the Sprint Goal.

In the end, who cares about what you worked on yesterday and what you are going to do today? What matters is, is your team moving the needle so that you can accomplish the Sprint Goal 100%. And, if not, what needs to happen today for you to be back on track?

From this point of view, it does not matter who speaks at the Daily Scrum. What matters is, as a team, are we on track to deliver the Sprint Goal and to complete all of the work in the Sprint Backlog, and if not, what do we do to achieve it?

Sometimes, it may be useful to use a different structure. My favorite is the PBI-by-PBI Review (or Walk the Wall) format where the team looks at the Sprint Backlog together (sometimes, this is the team board or the Kanban board the team is using to track the work for the Sprint). The team reviews each PBI that is still open on the Sprint Backlog and discusses its progress. The focus is on the work and what you need to do today to move it forward. This helps the team focus on the Sprint Goal and to take ownership of how to achieve it.

Our suggestion is: Everyone who is working on a work item during that Sprint should be updating the team. The update should be focused on the Sprint Goal. If the Product Owner or the Scrum Master are working on something that may impact the Sprint Goal, then they should provide an update as well.

For example, if the Scrum Master is working with the IT team to get access for a certain tool for the team, the Scrum Master should let everyone know if there is any progress on getting that access, and what they are going to do next to get it completed.

#40

CAN A DEVELOPER WORK ON MULTIPLE SCRUM TEAMS?

The Scrum Guide does not say that team members cannot work on multiple teams. However, Scrum does encourage the team members to work as one unit cohesively toward reaching the Sprint Goal. For the team to be successful in becoming self-managed and cross-functional, it is important to have dedicated team members. When your team members work on complex tasks, they often have to sync up with each other and if your team members are busy with other teams or projects, they begin to lose collaboration and communication.

We realize that sometimes, "ideal Scrum" does not equate to "real life." Team members may not be dedicated to one Scrum Team and may work on multiple teams and multiple projects at the same time. For them, this is just reality. And there is nothing wrong with it. However, there is a reason why Scrum recommends having dedicated team members: team members who work on multiple teams risk losing Focus and breaking their

Commitment (two Scrum Values).

When team members are multitasking, they often complain about working all the time and still not being able to finish tasks. When one project is in critical condition, the Developers tend to work on it, forgetting the other one. Priorities are hard to maintain, and so is focus. Also, the number of meetings that a Developer has to attend if they are part of multiple Scrum Teams doubles or triples depending on how many teams they belong to, leaving hardly any time for the work to be completed in each Sprint. They miss having that sense of accomplishment which leads to frustration, and which may impact the individual's and the team's morale.

Real life may be hard to change, but if you are aware of what you are losing by compromising on implementing Scrum in the proper way, at least you can put in place ways to limit the drawbacks.

REAL STORY

A hospital network company wanted to ideate the medical practice of the future. They put together a cross-functional team with team members from various parts of the business, and started working as a Scrum Team. Their job was to experiment with different physical layouts to learn what worked best, and what created the best customer experience. They redesigned the waiting area, the exam area, and the doctor's office, and tested different methods to provide information to the patient while in the space. They built prototypes using drywall, plywood, and cardboard, and iterated on multiple design ideas.

The team used Scrum with 2-week Sprints. The team members were not dedicated to the team: in fact, everyone had different responsibilities on a daily basis, and participated in this project only part-time.

After a couple of Sprints, it was clear that the team was not able to accomplish what they had set out to do in their Sprint Goal. Things continued to come up in their daily jobs, preventing them from focusing on the Sprint work. Also, they relied on external contractors to build up and to take down the drywall structures, and the 2-week Sprints were not long enough for the contractors to complete their work.

There was nothing these team members could do to address the non-dedicated nature of their work. We just had to live with it. What we changed, was the Sprint duration. We changed to 3-week Sprints, giving everyone (including the contractors) more time to complete their work.

Even with a longer Sprint, we kept the team's capacity the same, in effect, creating a buffer. This gave the team some slack in their plan, allowing them to deal with unexpected requests in their daily jobs and to still be able to complete the work of the Sprint.

#41

IS IT POSSIBLE TO COMBINE THE SCRUM MASTER ROLE WITH THE PRODUCT OWNER OR WITH THE DEVELOPER?

In our experience, when an individual plays more than one role on a Scrum Team, they are conflicted and become easily overwhelmed. Consider these combinations:

– **Scrum Master/Developer:** This is the most commonly found combination. As a Scrum Master, one of your responsibilities is to serve the team. If you are a Developer on that team, how are you going to help your team members when you are absorbed in your development work that you committed to during that Sprint? If instead, you are able to help your team, your own development work might get affected and delayed. How do you coach yourself when you do something that violates a Scrum value?

– **Scrum Master/Product Owner:** The Scrum Master is team focused; the Product Owner is business focused. During the Sprint, your Developers need help in resolving a few impediments. At the same time, you have meetings with your clients and then another one in the afternoon with your Marketing Director about some new requirements. Who are you going to prioritize, your team or your Stakeholders? I think we know the answer to that one.

– **Product Owner/Developer:** As a Product Owner, you are supposed to get estimates on the work items from the Developers. But, if you are both a Product Owner and a Developer, you may ignore the rest of the team's input and just estimate the PBIs on your own. Also, as the Product Owner, you are responsible for prioritizing the Product Backlog based on customer and business values. But, if you are also a Developer, you may decide to prioritize something that you like working on, rather than a PBI that is more valuable but harder to do.

These are all examples of possible conflicts that may arise when multiple Scrum roles are combined in the same person. The end result is ineffective and is a potential conflict of interest. When someone tries to perform two roles, neither of the roles gets the attention it requires, and both get diluted.

We are not saying that this cannot be done. It is a typical trade-off between "ideal Scrum" and "real life." Sometimes, two roles are combined, and that is the way in which the team operates (at least, in the short term, until a proper solution is found). By being aware of the compromise and possible conflicts, you may be able to take precautions to avoid the drawbacks. And, work with your Stakeholders to get the support your Scrum Team needs in order to have dedicated roles and to become more effective.

#42

WHO DOES THE REPORTING, STATUS UPDATES TO THE SENIOR MANAGEMENT, AND SO FORTH?

The Scrum Guide does not have any guidance on that. In our experience, we have seen the following:

The Product Owner does the reporting to the senior management and to Stakeholders, since the Product Owner interacts and has a continuous relationship with them. To provide updates, the Product Owner may share the Release Plan and the Roadmaps, whenever needed, and any decisions they have made on the Product Backlog and on its priorities.

Throughout the Sprint, the Scrum Artifacts provide **Transparency** and help to track progress of the ongoing work. The Developers update the Sprint Backlog, the team board, the Burn-down Chart and any other information radiator they use to track the progress of their work. Stakeholders are encouraged to review the Artifacts to stay updated on the progress of the Sprint and on the overall Product Goal.

By design, Scrum offers an event that is dedicated to provide updates to the Stakeholders. That event is the Sprint Review. The Sprint Review is more than just a "demo." The Scrum Team and the Stakeholders can also inspect the environment (team situation, market changes, competition, etc.), the Product Backlog and its upcoming priorities, the Release Plan, where the team is in the Roadmap, and so forth.

There is no need for additional meetings when the Sprint Review is used effectively as it is designed. Any Stakeholder who wants to get updates about the work that the Scrum Team is doing, should be invited to participate in the Sprint Review. By attending the Sprint Review, Stakeholders get to review what the team has developed so far, to contribute to the future direction of the product, and to provide feedback. They learn about the overall progress and the various impediments the team faces, and they may offer support in overcoming them. Effective Sprint Review meetings help to build trust between the Stakeholders and Scrum Team members.

This leads to the most important point, a typical anti-pattern that we often see taking place in Scrum Teams. And that pertains to the role of the Scrum Master in providing status updates.

The role of the Scrum Master is not to act as the secretary of the team, or to update the artifacts, or to provide updates to Stakeholders. In fact, the Scrum Master should do none of these. As just seen, the Developers can update the artifacts and track the progress of the work during the Sprint. They do not need a secretary to do the updates for them. And the Product Owner can interact with the Stakeholders and answer any questions they may have.

Instead, the Scrum Master should focus on their role as a coach.

They can coach the Developers and the Product Owner on what techniques to use to track the work, how to share artifacts, how to create transparency with the Stakeholders, why it is important to have Stakeholders participate in Sprint Reviews, and so forth. By acting as a coach (rather than doing the work) the Scrum Master can ensure that over time, the Developers and the Product Owner on the Scrum Team grow as individuals and as professionals, strengthening their relationships with Stakeholders and creating trust.

#43

CAN UNFINISHED/ PARTIALLY FINISHED ITEMS BE ROLLED OVER ONTO THE NEXT SPRINT; CAN WE GET CREDIT FOR THE WORK DONE IN THE CURRENT SPRINT?

Rolling automatically all of the unfinished/partially finished items into the following Sprint, is something we strongly advise against. Those items should be moved back to the Product Backlog and reprioritized by the Product Owner. And, the team should not get any partial credit for partial work. Let us explain why:

At Sprint Planning, the Developers, working together with the Product Owner, create the Sprint Backlog and commit to the Sprint Goal. They are setting the expectation that by the end of the Sprint, 100% of the Sprint Goal and of the Sprint Backlog representing that goal, will be completed.

This is a forecast not an absolute commitment.

In fact, it should not be treated in an absolute way, so that if the team fails to achieve it, everyone gets penalized: "You said you would complete 100% of the work, and you only did 99% of it, so now you are fired!" That is not the sort of environment we want to create.

On the other hand, the forecast should be respected because if you set the expectation that it does not matter what the Developers actually accomplish or not during the Sprint, then why even set up a Sprint Goal in the first place? I can imagine someone saying: "Poor folks, we appreciate good intentions. You only completed 10% of your commitment, no worries; here is the partial credit and by the way, here is also a bonus for your goodwill." This does not work.

So, the commitment of the Developers to achieve the Sprint Goal and to complete the work selected in the Sprint Backlog must be treated with respect. This supports the values of **Commitment**, of **Courage** to do difficult work, and of **Focus** on achieving the Sprint Goal.

Now, we all understand that reality is different from the best of plans. Things happen. And even the best teams may not be able to complete 100% of the work they committed to doing. We understand that. The point is, set the condition for the team to commit to their work and to be able to execute it fully 100% in the Sprint, and if from time to time they cannot complete it, so be it. This is way better than taking on too much work, overcommitting yourself, and basically setting the condition to never complete all of the work you selected for the Sprint.

REAL STORY

Ever seen a team say: "We completed 65 points this Sprint, out of 85 points we had selected (76% completion), and that was the HIGHEST velocity we ever achieved?"

I once worked with a scaled team (multiple Agile teams working on the same project) where every team would say something like this at the Sprint Review, and they expected people to congratulate them. Sprint after Sprint.

My question was: "If this was the HIGHEST you ever achieved so far, it means you never accomplished 100% of your commitment. Why is that happening?"

When we started looking at how the teams operated, it became clear that the Product Owner was giving the work to the Developers without any conversation about the actual capacity for the Sprint. They overcommitted all the time, causing an insane amount of stress for the team, of incomplete work, and quality issues as a result.

My coaching to the team was: "Go slow to go far." Select only the work you can reasonably complete in the Sprint, get all of it done, and then if you have spare time ask the Product Owner for more. This is the Teams that Finish Early Accelerate Faster pattern[1] in action.

SPRINT YOUR WAY TO SCRUM

When some work items are not fully done by the end of the Sprint, these items are not included in the Increment, and simply go back to the Product Backlog. It does not matter if they are 50% done, or 99% done. If they are not done, they go back to the Product Backlog.

Next, the Developers should have a discussion about those items with the Product Owner and help the Product Owner understand why it makes sense for the team to finish those items in the following Sprint (or maybe not). The Product Owner may have a list of prioritized items that may supersede those unfinished/partially finished items. After the discussion, the Product Owner takes into account the various scenarios and then prioritizes the items to be worked on in the following Sprint.

The team also does not get any partial credit for partial work. It is all or nothing. All incomplete work goes back to the Product Backlog. I have seen many teams getting upset over not getting credit for the partial work done during that Sprint. By not giving partial credit for incomplete work, you hold the Developers accountable for selecting the right amount of work (within the team's capacity) and for completing it (Commitment). The Developers will get credit for the full work item in a future Sprint when the work item is finally fully completed.

You may say that this may disrupt the team's velocity and introduce high variability. You are right; it may, and there are two ways to deal with it:

1. Make sure your work items are small. Working with smaller items has the advantage of increasing the flow of work in the team (more work gets completed in a given interval of time) and it reduces the variability on velocity for unfinished work.

2. You can use the average velocity over the last three Sprints. This offsets any dips or jumps in velocity due to incomplete work.

When incomplete work piles up during every Sprint, we invite the team to hold a Retrospective and to discuss what is causing the work to be incomplete. Often, there is some structure for the team that is missing or that is not working as it should. For example, the Developers tend to commit to too much work (higher than their capacity in the Sprint) or they do not have a buffer in place (to create slack and to deal with unexpected events during the Sprint). Use the Retrospective to figure out why the team was unable to finish the work and to put in place action items to improve.

Another question we often get is about estimates: "Should we re -estimate the incomplete work items to account for only the work remaining, before selecting them for the next Sprint?" There are two schools of thought here, the "Re-estimate" and the "No Re-estimate."

- **Re-estimate:** Velocity measures are more accurate as the new estimate reflects the remaining work on the PBI. Con: The additional time spent to re-estimate the item may not be worth the effort.

- **No Re-estimate:** No waste of time in re-estimating. Con: the next Sprint's velocity increases because you get credit for the full work item (even if only partial work was completed in the Sprint). Solution: Average the velocity over the last three Sprints.

In general, we prefer to avoid unnecessary complexity in the process. However, you can use one method or the other based on your team's preference.

REFERENCES

1. Teams that Finish Early Accelerate Faster: A Pattern Language for High Performing Scrum Teams https://www.scruminc.com/wp-content/uploads/2014/05/teamsthatfinishearlyacceleratefaster.pdf

#44

CAN THE BUSINESS ANALYST PLAY THE ROLE OF THE PRODUCT OWNER?

The Product Owner has a set of responsibilities, while the Business Analyst is a title we give a person on a team. Anyone can play the role of a Product Owner as long as they fulfill the responsibilities and develop the skills. In my experience, I have seen many Business Analysts play the role of a Product Owner and be successful. However, it is important that the organization respects the authority of that role.

Consider this real-life conversation with a senior manager:

Mgr: "Our Business Analyst will act as the Product Owner on the Scrum Team."

Bonsy: "How did you arrive at that conclusion?"

Mgr: "It is easy, he will maintain the Product Backlog, attend various Scrum Meetings throughout the Sprint, be available to the team to answer their questions, provide clarification on the requirements, and basically, be there for the Scrum Team."

Bonsy: "That is great in terms of availability! How about authority? Consider this scenario: A developer reaches out to that Business Analyst and lets them know that out of the 10 User Stories forecasted for that Sprint, they can only deliver 8 because of some unforeseen impediments. The Developer wants to know which 2 User Stories can be dropped off from the Sprint. Will your Business Analyst be able to make that decision?"

Mgr: "Not really, he will reach out to me and I will decide which 2 User Stories can be dropped and he can relay it back to the team."

Bonsy: "So he is a proxy! The Business Analyst does not have any authority to make decisions that a Product Owner should be able to make during a Sprint! How is that effective?"

Given the short lengths of our Sprints, how effective is this whole back-and-forth relaying of information? If the Business Analyst acts as the Product Owner for the team, they should not be a proxy for someone else. They should have the authority and the availability to play the role of the Product Owner effectively.

#45

IS IT OK TO ESTIMATE IN TIME?

You are free to estimate however your team sees fit. Scrum is a framework; it is not prescriptive. If estimating your User Stories in time works for your team, go for it. During the Retrospective, bring it up and check how everyone feels about estimating in time.

Studies show that time estimates tend to suffer from "optimism bias," that is, we tend to underestimate the time it takes to do things. Time estimates show a high error rate and a variance. As a result, time estimates are less reliable compared to estimates based on effort.

Every estimate is always a guess (we try to predict the future and no one can really do it accurately). Estimates are neither precise nor accurate. There is always an implied level of error in every estimate; they are guesses after all. The goal is to learn to make reliable estimates, that is, those that have a lower level of variability compared to reality (more accurate and with smaller errors).

When we estimate in time, we assume a false level of precision. And then we complain that the deadlines we set are not realistic. Instead, using estimates based on effort allows you to look more closely at how much work there is, how complex the work is, how much do you know or not know about it, and how unpredictable it is. These components all together represent the effort.

We recommend the use of **effort** for estimation (effort is a combination of how much work there is, of complexity, of lack of knowledge, and of unknowns), and stay away from time.

Also, estimates in time, tend to provide a false expectation of delivery dates without taking into account the team's velocity. And this causes greater frustration when the expected date is not met.

I was once coaching a team where frequently there would be three different team members working on the same User Story, and it was tricky estimating everyone's exact minutes and hours spent on each task (time). Therefore, the team decided to give the estimation based on effort a try. Scrum encourages experimentation.

As Scrum Masters, we are here to serve our teams. If you see that your teams are struggling in estimating User Stories in absolute values (time), then maybe it is time to look into other formats and techniques that will help your teams.

#46

HOW DO I KNOW IF THE SCRUM MASTER IS DOING A GOOD JOB?

There are many ways you can assess if you have an effective Scrum Master on your team. Ultimately, the job of the Scrum Master is to help the Scrum Team learn and become effective at implementing Scrum. The Scrum Master should be able to take the team from wherever they are and to make it a highly performing team.

Consider these outcomes:

– **Team Happiness:** is the team performing with a high level of trust in each other, support, openness, and personal satisfaction? Measuring the *Team Happiness* metric is one of the patterns of successful Scrum Teams[1].

– **Increased velocity:** is the team's velocity increasing over time, as a result of better ways of doing the work and continuous improvement activities (e.g., action items from the Retrospective)?

– **Quality of work:** is the quality of the work produced by the Scrum Team increasing over time? This can be measured by the number of defects, the number of incomplete work items in a Sprint (due to failed tests), adherence to the Definition of Done, the amount of technical debt accumulated, and the complaints received from the customers of your product.

How the Scrum Master helps the Scrum Team achieve these outcomes, varies from team to team. However, a Scrum Master can use any of the following activities to identify areas of impact and to help the team improve:

– **Scrum Teacher** – Does your Scrum Master understand the concepts of the Scrum framework? Can your Scrum Master teach Scrum effectively? Do they use different techniques and practices to impart knowledge about Scrum?

– **Coach** – Are they effectively able to coach team members and to help them improve their understanding of the various elements of the framework? Is the Scrum Master coaching the team members so that they grow personally and professionally? As a coach, is your Scrum Master providing constructive feedback to the team on their implementing the Scrum framework?

– **Facilitator** – Is your Scrum Master effectively facilitating meetings? Do they assist and make things easy for the team by using various facilitation techniques? Are they able to address issues openly and to help resolve them fruitfully? Are your teams attending and conducting Scrum events even when the Scrum Master is unavailable?

– **Good Communicator** – Is the Scrum Master effectively able to communicate with the team as well as with the others who collaborate with the Scrum Team? The Scrum Master should be able to communicate well verbally as well as in writing.

– **Impediment Remover** – How successful is your Scrum Master in helping the team remove blockers that come in your team's way? Are they providing support to the Developers in removing impediments?

– **Focus** – Is your Scrum Master tactfully able to shield your team from constant interruptions during the Sprint? Is the Scrum Master coaching the team on the value of Focus to avoid working on too many things at once or on tasks unrelated to the Sprint Goal?

– **Scrum Patterns** – Is the Scrum Master helping the team adopt successful patterns? Examples: *Interrupt Buffer*, reserving capacity for unplanned work; *Yesterday's Weather* pattern, using past performance indicators (team's velocity) to establish a Sprint's capacity; *Swarming*, inviting the Developers to focus their work on one item at a time and work on it all together, especially in case of bottlenecks[1, 2].

– **Encourage Experimentation** – Is your Scrum Master always encouraging team members to try new techniques and ideas, giving them support, and creating an environment they need in order to try those new ideas?

– **Address Issues Openly** – Is your Scrum Master helping the team address the "Elephant in the Room"? Are they openly discussing sticky issues in the team that everyone is aware of but that no one wants to bring up? Is your Scrum Master encouraging self-management or cross-functionality on your teams?

– **Technical Practices** – Is the Scrum Master inviting the team to adopt and to improve their engineering practices, reducing technical debt, and improving the quality of the work? Does the team have and respect a Definition of Done?

These are questions that you may ask about your Scrum Master (or, if you are a Scrum Master, ask yourself): you might possibly identify areas of improvement.

REFERENCES

1. Scrum Pattern Group https://www.scrumplop.org/
2. Teams that Finish Early Accelerate Faster: A Pattern Language for High Performing Scrum Teams https://www.scruminc.com/wp-content/uploads/2014/05/teamsthatfinishearlyacceleratefaster.pdf

#47

WHY DO WE NEED A FULL-TIME SCRUM MASTER?

Scrum Masters help build skills and improve the performance of both individuals and the team. They provide a structure that helps the team adapt to changing circumstances. They help identify the gaps and opportunities, and encourage the team to do what needs to be done better. As a servant leader, they create an environment in which the team members freely share their knowledge, questions, mistakes, and successes so that they together, reflect and improve as a team. A Scrum Master builds a culture of trust and a strong relationship within the team.

Everyone who is looking to improve themselves in any field, wants feedback on how they can improve. Scrum Masters provide feedback on how the team is doing and how they can become better. Even professional athletes and Olympians have coaches who help them improve their skills and techniques. Having a full-time Scrum Master for the team ensures that there is a person whose job is to help the team perform consistently while maintaining sustainable pace.

As a servant-leader, they elicit the strengths and knowledge of their team members – individually and as a team. They create an environment in which the team can focus on the overarching goal, prevent micromanaging, and give the team an opportunity to prove their competency.

Additionally, they also:

– Teach the Scrum framework and support the Scrum Team in adopting it.

– Facilitate various meetings and conversations as needed.

– Shield the team from interruptions, help the team focus on the work, and support the team in removing impediments.

– Coach anyone who interacts with your Scrum team about this different way of working.

– Coach the Product Owner and Developers on practices and behaviors that improve performance and quality of the work.

As you can see, a Scrum Master has lots to do during the Sprint, and a focused Scrum Master helps the team mature faster in using the Scrum framework and in improving their productivity.

As Geoff Watts (also a CST from Scrum Alliance) mentions in his book "Scrum Mastery"[1], a good Scrum Master can serve two teams at the same time, but a great Scrum Master serves only one Scrum team.

REFERENCES

1. "Scrum Mastery", by Geoff Watts

48

HOW IS THE PROJECT MANAGER ROLE DIFFERENT FROM A SCRUM MASTER ?

When an organization adopts Scrum, the Project Manager's responsibilities are divided among the three Scrum roles: Product Owner, Scrum Master, and Developers. Here are some examples:

– Before, the Project Manager did requirements management, Stakeholder and Client/Customer management, created Roadmaps, managed the budget of the project, and decided on the release dates of the projects. Now, the Product Owner does all of those activities.

– Before, the Project Manager kept the day-to-day dashboards up-to-date throughout the project and tracked the progress of the work. Now, the Developers ensure that the Sprint Backlog is up-to-date and visible to everyone, and track the progress of

SPRINT YOUR WAY TO SCRUM

their own work during the Sprint.

– Before, the Project Manager was in charge of keeping the team focused during the project, shielding them from interruptions, removing any impediments that came in their way, and creating an environment in which the team successfully met their goals. Now the Scrum Master does all of those things.

The Scrum Master does not replace a Project Manager as the two jobs are very different, however, some of the responsibilities are the same. Some of the high-level differences are as follows:

– The Project Manager is more project focused versus the Scrum Master who is more team focused.

– The Project Manager is more of a manager of a team versus the Scrum Master who is a servant leader who serves the team in improving performance and in achieving their goal.

– The Project Manager's mindset is usually about assigning tasks and tracking the work versus the Scrum Master who is about encouraging the team to self-organize and to take ownership of their own tasks.

– Many Project Managers are used to people reporting to them versus the Product Owner and Developers who do not usually report to the Scrum Master as there is no hierarchy on the Scrum team.

So now the question changes to, "What happens to the Project Manager's role in organizations that are implementing the Scrum framework?"

Based on my experience, the Project Manager's role is evolving. Many Project Managers relate a lot with the Product Owner's role as they feel that they are already doing most of what a Product Owner does and they decide to become Product Owners. Some Project Managers are natural servant leaders and they choose to become Scrum Masters.

#49

MY TEAM IS UNINTERESTED IN THE RETROSPECTIVES, AND, WHEN WE DO THEM, I AM THE ONLY ONE WHO TALKS. SHOULD I STOP DOING THEM?

First, I would try to find out why the team is disinterested. Do they think it is a waste of time? Do they understand the purpose of Retrospectives? If not with a Retrospective, how does the team identify opportunities for improvement (*Kaizen*)?

Here are a few suggestions to make the Retrospective more interesting:

– One way to engage the team is to get their buy-in. Help everyone understand the purpose of this event and the expected outcome.

– At the start of the meeting, ask one of the Developers to kick-off the conversation with something that they wanted to share or that they observed during the Sprint. Doing this instead of it always being the Scrum Master's job to facilitate, helps to change the format.

– Maybe begin the meeting by watching a fun video that a team member may have come across which lightens the mood.

– Many teams conduct their Retrospective over their meals (virtual teams all eat lunch together at their own desks with the camera on). As an alternative, the team can go out and have a drink at the end of the day together, and use that happy-hour to discuss how their Sprint went and what they can improve in the next one.

REAL STORY

On one of my teams, a team member was feeling low during a particular Retrospective since he had only worked on production issues during that Sprint and did not get a chance to work on any new exciting features. To make him feel better, the team decided to let him choose which idea the team should work on improving in the next Sprint.

The team was looking out for one another.

Another important tip for the Retrospective, is to change the format or structure often. Asking, "What worked/what did not work" at every Retrospective, can quickly become repetitive or feel stagnant. How many new insights can you come up with by answering the same questions?

The suggestion is to change the format – something you can potentially do at each Retrospective. For example, do a Plus/Delta exercise once, then at the next use the Speedboat exercise, and then use the Genie of the Lamp. These are just examples; you may create your own list of favorite exercises. The invitation is to spend some time experimenting with different exercises and formats, and find your favorite ways to run the Retrospective.

For ideas, we recommend reading "Project Retrospectives"[1] and "Agile Retrospectives: Making Good Teams Great"[2]. Also, great resources for ideas on retrospective design are in various websites, including Tasty Cupcakes[3] and Retromat[4].

REFERENCES

1. "Project Retrospectives" by Norman Kerth
2. "Agile Retrospectives: Making Good Teams Great" by Esther Derby and Diana Larsen
3. Tasty Cupcakes http://tastycupcakes.org/tag/retrospective/
4. Retromat https://retromat.org/

#50

WHO OWNS THE SPRINT BACKLOG?

The Sprint Backlog is a plan by and for the Developers that is created during Sprint Planning. It includes both the list of PBIs selected for the Sprint ("What" the team is working on) and an action plan to execute the work ("How" the team is doing the work). The value of the Sprint Backlog lies in aligning everyone on the Scrum Team around what the Developers are going to work on and in creating transparency on how the work is being executed.

The Sprint Backlog is owned by the Developers on the Scrum Team, and it is their responsibility to maintain it during the Sprint. It is updated throughout the Sprint to reflect the work completed, changes to the plan, any new work added, and so on. The Sprint Backlog should always be visible to everyone, as it is a real-time snapshot of the work the Developers are doing throughout the Sprint.

We offer a few tips to make sure your team properly selects and manages the Sprint Backlog:

- When creating the Sprint Backlog, the Product Owner is responsible for providing the priorities on the work. The Developers are responsible for determining the amount of work they can select for the Sprint. Use historical velocity (the *Yesterday's Weather* pattern[1]) to determine the available capacity for the Sprint, and to limit the amount of work selected at or below capacity[2].

- Leave a buffer in your plan. One of the most common problems that Scrum teams face is unexpected events. These could be production issues that need to be fixed right away, new requests for work that are added to the Sprint Backlog in the middle of the Sprint, or someone on the team suddenly missing a few days of work reducing the available capacity. The Interrupt Buffer is a Scrum pattern that allows teams to manage unexpected events with limited disruption to their planned work. Research at Carnegie Mellon and 20 years of experience with Scrum teams has shown that teams that plan for interruptions do significantly better than teams that do not, even when they experience no interruptions[3].

- As you create your plan for executing the work in the Sprint Backlog, consider any dependencies you may have (within the work you have selected for the Sprint or with outside teams). Prioritize solving the dependencies first. The *Dependencies First* pattern recognizes that dependencies pose constraints on the team's ability to execute the work and they should be solved first. Ideally, the team should plan to address all dependencies in the first half of the Sprint[1].

- The Developers are responsible for tracking the progress of their work throughout the Sprint. At least daily, during the Daily Scrum, the Developers inspect the Sprint Backlog to review the progress they are making toward completing the work and achieving the Sprint Goal. Update the Sprint Backlog correspondingly, and use tools like the Burndown Chart to visualize and to track the progress of the work.

- Developers are also responsible for raising any impediments that may be in their way, preventing them from completing the work. By raising the impediment, other team members can help solve the problem, or they can ask the Scrum Master for additional support.

REFERENCES

1. Scrum Pattern Group https://www.scrumplop.org/

2. "Velocity, Capacity, or Load?" - https://www.5dvision.com/post/velocity-capacity-load/

3. Teams that Finish Early Accelerate Faster: A Pattern Language for High Performing Scrum Teams https://www.scruminc.com/wp-content/uploads/2014/05/teamsthatfinishhearlyacceleratefaster.pdf

BONSY YELSANGI, CST

Bonsy Yelsangi is a Certified Scrum Trainer (CST) and an Agile Coach. She has worked in a variety of industries, including media, remote managed services, luxury real estate, aviation, automotive, and private wealth management. Bonsy's IT background includes roles as QA Manager, Scrum Master, and Agile Coach for Waterfall and Agile teams.

She is the founder and CEO of Attain Agility, an organization that helps create an environment for teams that will help them – you guessed it – Attain Agility!

Bonsy is devoted to creating energized and excited teams that delight their customers and that inspire others. She is passionate about helping teams and organizations discover the Scrum/Kanban/Lean mash-ups that enable focused, flexible, and fast delivery of products. Bonsy provides Agile-focused training and coaching to companies ranging from late-stage startups, to large corporations; she is adept in administering all aspects of project management, as well as providing authentic leadership in order to create effective teams.

She educates people at all levels of the organization, from executives and leaders, to developers, PMs, BAs, and others working on project delivery. As a Scrum Trainer, she is known for her engaging style of training in person, as well as in the virtual world.

https://www.linkedin.com/in/bonsy-yelsangi-b86317102/

VALERIO ZANINI, CST, CPIT

Valerio Zanini is a Certified Scrum Trainer (CST) and a Certified Product Innovation Trainer (CPIT). As a Scrum and Product Management Trainer, he works with organizations worldwide to spark the adoption of Agile and Product practices.

With more than 20 years of professional experience spanning software development, system integration, design thinking, and product innovation, he is the founder and CEO of the product innovation firm 5D Vision, with offices in Washington, DC. He provides consulting and training to organizations of any size, helping them become more innovative with product mastery, with agile methodologies, and with design thinking.

He was a Director of Product Development at Capital One where he led digital transformation initiatives for the retail bank division and transformed the manner in which customers interact with bankers. Before Capital One, Valerio was the cofounder and CEO of Goozex (sold in 2012), a Systems Engineer at Cisco, and the cofounder of one of the first web development companies in Italy.

He is a Certified Scrum Trainer (CST) with Scrum Alliance, a SAFe Program Consultant (SPC), and a Certified Product Innovation Trainer (CPIT) with Spark Engine. He holds an MBA from the University of Maryland, and an MS/BS in Electronic and Computer Engineering from the University of Rome.

He is also the author of *Deliver Great Products that Customers Love: The Guide to Product Management for Innovators, Leaders, and Entrepreneurs* (Washington, DC, 2018).

https://www.linkedin.com/in/vzanini/

NOTES

NOTES

We hope you enjoyed it!

We plant one tree for every copy sold

We are happy to work with ForestPlanet and their
network of tree planting partners to implement
our tree planting program. Please
visit ForestPlanet to learn more about this
amazing organization. ForestPlanet.org

ForestPlanet

Made in United States
Orlando, FL
26 January 2024